The Secret Life of

BIRDS OF PREY

The Secret Life of

BIRDS OF PREY

Feathers, Fury and Friendship

CHLOÉ VALERIE HARMSWORTH

WHITE OWL
AN IMPRINT OF PEN & SWORD BOOKS LTD.
YORKSHIRE – PHILADELPHIA

First published in Great Britain in 2023 by
White Owl
An imprint of
Pen & Sword Books Ltd
Yorkshire - Philadelphia

ISBN 978 1 39909 324 8

A CIP catalogue record for this book is available from the British Library.

Cover image credits:
Main front cover image: Adobe Stock: andyastbury
Red kite image: Chloé Valerie Harmsworth
Back cover: Adobe Stock: romantiche
Back flap of cover: Adobe Stock: mzphoto11
(Recto footer image in book is a red kite from a photo by Russell Sherriff.
Verso is a white-tailed eagle from a photo by Daniel/Adobe Stock)

Typeset in 11/14 pts Cormorant Infant
by SJmagic DESIGN SERVICES, India.
Printed and bound in India by Replika Press Pvt. Ltd.

Pen & Sword Books Ltd incorporates the imprints of Pen & Sword Books Archaeology, Atlas, Aviation, Battleground, Discovery, Family History, History, Maritime, Military, Naval, Politics, Railways, Select, Transport, True Crime, Fiction, Frontline Books, Leo Cooper, Praetorian Press, Seaforth Publishing, Wharncliffe and White Owl.

For a complete list of Pen & Sword titles please contact

PEN & SWORD BOOKS LIMITED
George House, Units 12 & 13, Beevor Street, Off Pontefract Road,
Barnsley, South Yorkshire, S71 1HN, England
E-mail: enquiries@pen-and-sword.co.uk
Website: www.pen-and-sword.co.uk

or

PEN AND SWORD BOOKS
1950 Lawrence Rd, Havertown, PA 19083, USA
E-mail: uspen-and-sword@casematepublishers.com
Website: www.penandswordbooks.com

Contents

Male kestrel. (© Sue Slater)

Foreword

It has always seemed strange to me that birds of prey (also known as raptors), with their important role in maintaining healthy ecosystems, can be simultaneously revered and despised by humans.

Thirty years ago when I began my career in the conservation of these birds, I chose to work overseas because I thought that was where the threats to these species were most significant and where I thought my efforts would have the most impact. But when I returned to the UK to take a job studying golden eagles in Scotland, I was shocked to discover that our birds of prey are under immense threat too, generally as a result of ignorance.

After the extinction of some species (for example the white-tailed eagle) and the severe range contraction of others (such as the hen harrier, golden eagle and buzzard) in previous centuries through heavy persecution, society's perception of birds of prey has since improved and legal protection has been given to the birds. A number of successful reintroduction projects have returned certain species to their former haunts (including the white-tailed eagle, osprey and red kite), and these projects have been widely supported and celebrated by the public.

However, horrifyingly, our birds of prey are still illegally killed, either by poisoning, shooting or trapping. This mostly happens on land managed for game bird shooting because birds of prey are perceived as a threat to the game birds. Every year there are news reports of eagles and buzzards being found poisoned, peregrines and red kites being shot, and hen harriers and goshawks being trapped and bludgeoned to death. This is happening on such a scale that it is affecting the population and distribution of many of our bird of prey species.

That some people, in a so-called progressive place like the UK, still refer to these birds as 'vermin' is astonishing and embarrassing. It is undoubtedly aggravated by sections of the media, who demonise these birds to grab headlines, for example claiming that towns are being 'terrorised' by red kites grabbing food out of people's hands. This does nothing to educate the public about the benefits of birds of prey to our environment and also does not help to stop those intent on killing them.

This misunderstanding and misrepresentation of birds of prey is why Chloë's book is so important; any book that sets out to educate and inform the public about these special birds is very welcome. I hope that it will inspire readers to go out and watch birds of prey, wherever that may be, to enjoy the thrill of a sighting and develop an appreciation that they are a vital part of the UK's biodiversity.

Dr Ruth Tingay

Author of Raptor Persecution UK blog (raptorpersecutionuk.org) and co-director of Wild Justice (wildjustice.org.uk)

Acknowledgements

My heartfelt thanks go to: Stefan Glosby (for your love, support and proofreading!), Claudia Harflett (for our life-enriching adventures), Amy Burgess (for your friendship, loyalty and getting me through 2022), Tina Hyde, Jax Burgoyne and Josephine Ketskemety (for the same reasons). Finally, to Rose and Dave Newbold, for lending me your camera and inviting me to Mull! I am so grateful to you all.

Thanks also to the photographers who were kind enough to let me use their stunning images so that readers can be awed by the beauty of these birds: Rose and Dave Newbold (again!), Graham Parkinson, Patrick Wainwright, Andrew Steele, Sue Slater, Barry Madden, Barry Jackson, Russell Sherriff, George Cook, Bob Cooper, Pete Woods, Mick Brockington, Steve Elwell, Donna Robinson, Karen Blow and Ralph Lightman. A particular shout-out to Howard Vaughan for helping me to source some of these photographs and to Barry Trevis for all the conservation work he does for Hertfordshire's birds of prey.

Likewise to the story-tellers, who assisted me in breathing joy and delight into this book: James Aldred, for being so obliging and generous; Joe Harkness, my fellow devotee of nature therapy; Kate Stephenson, with whom I loved working on our *Connections with Nature* book; Steve Shand, who I met at the launch event for said book; Angela Foxwood, with whom I bonded at the 2014 D.H. Lawrence Poetry Prize ceremony; Howard Vaughan, who advised me on where to see marsh harriers when I met him at Rainham Marshes; Sandi Monger and Craig Dibb, my 'Insta' mates; Anna Gilbert-Falconer, who I serendipitously stumbled across on the same platform; and Daniel 'Mullman' Brooks, who I met whale (and then eagle!) watching on Mull.

Last but not least, thanks to Ruth Tingay for providing an excellent foreword, that perfectly opens this book, and means so much to me.

And thanks to all the birds, of course. Especially you, Roger.

Chloé Valerie Harmsworth
Nature writer, poet, photographer and artist

chloevalerienatureart.wordpress.com
Instagram @chloevalerienatureart

Introduction

Thank you for picking up this book. Inside you will find information on 13 of our UK birds of prey.

Before we get started, it's important to note a few things. Firstly, that I have not included owls. Some think they ought to be under the label 'birds of prey'; others don't. To me, owls are a subject by themselves, and they belong to their own group: *Strigiformes*. I would love to write about them one day, but you won't find them here.

The term 'bird of prey' is often used interchangeably with 'raptor', and I have decided to use the former throughout for consistency. (Any references to the latter are in error.) There are also birds such as the honey buzzard and Montagu's harrier that are not mentioned; these are summer visitors to the UK, in very low numbers.

The chapters, which cover each bird of prey (or in the case of the harrier chapter, two), are divided into the following sections: history and current situation; description, characteristics and behaviour; habitat, nesting habits and breeding; a personal story; where to see them. My aim is to introduce you to these extraordinary birds, describe them and their habits, give pointers on where you can see them, and explain the impact of persecution on them and how they are making a comeback.

This is not an in-depth textbook; it is an opener to the subject. Please consider it as such and let it inspire you. Whether you already know a bit or are a total newcomer, this book should increase your appreciation and knowledge of these stunning birds with straightforward facts, snippets of history, cultural references, touches of folklore and poetic moments. I hope it will be a springboard for you to explore the subject further, in whatever direction you wish, and motivate you to donate a little time or money to the conservation charities and sanctuaries that help these birds. (See the *Useful resources* section towards the end of the book.)

As I wrote this book, I considered how to make it as engaging as possible. Photography is, of course, key to bringing the subject to life; through images readers can see up close how beautiful these enigmatic, fleeting creatures are. And wherever I could, I used photos from photographers I knew or had made contact with, rather than going straight to a photo library. This is because I wanted a collaborative quality to the book, and it was delightful how excited photographers were to contribute. These exchanges made the process of writing (a frequently isolating endeavour) less solitary. And I wanted more of that.

Having written wildlife articles for magazines and websites, I have found the most successful ones are usually those in which I express my love and enthusiasm. For example, I have waxed lyrical about how special red kites are to me, and this obsession has ultimately led to me writing this book. Readers crave personal points of view and real experiences, not just reams of facts, so it went without saying that I would incorporate these into my book.

I started with my red kite chapter (naturally), describing a few experiences and conveying my adoration with a poem. I'm certain that this individual perspective and emotions show the beneficial effect wildlife can have on our lives. It gives so much to us. When we realise this, we will care, and by caring we will be moved to protect nature and give back to it.

In the summer of 2021, I met Aida the beautiful red kite at Huxley's, a wonderful bird of prey centre in West Sussex. Seeing my passion, the volunteers kindly let me hold her. Here I am speechless with emotion and locking eyes with her during this special, unforgettable moment. (Photo kindly taken by Claudia Harflett)

That's when it hit me: I could write about a lot of the birds based on my own encounters, but not all of them. Should I run around the UK trying to find them all? I didn't think so. Not only would that be impractical, but it wasn't the way I wanted to go about this book. Faced with this dilemma, I realised there was another option. This was the perfect opportunity to bring other people in, to have other voices in the mix!

Enraptured by this idea, I approached various people hoping that they would want to share their bird of prey memories with me. And thankfully, they did! Soon I had a team consisting of James Aldred, Joe Harkness, Kate Stephenson, Angela Foxwood, Howard Vaughan, Steve Shand, Sandi Monger, Craig Dibb, Anna Gilbert-Falconer and Daniel Brooks. Certain individuals I knew through the wonderful community of nature lovers on Instagram, and others I had met in person, or worked with before. (Find out more in the Acknowledgements.)

I am incredibly grateful to these humans for their beautiful words that relate their connection to a specific bird of prey. I truly believe that their stories add something special to this book, making the subject even more engaging and accessible. Finally, these examples provide additional evidence to support my theory that birds of prey are life-changing for those who open their eyes and hearts to them.

May this book encourage you to form your own connections – out in nature, through books, via the webcam, or in whatever way works for you.

Enjoy!

General information and advice

This chapter gives an overview of the bird species included under the umbrella term 'birds of prey'. It describes certain overarching features, general points and things to be aware of, and also provides useful advice.

To begin with, here is a list of the birds described in this book.

Falconidae (falcons)
- Peregrine falcon
- Kestrel
- Merlin
- Hobby

Accipitridae (kites, hawks and eagles)
- Buzzard
- Red kite
- Hen harrier
- Marsh harrier
- Goshawk
- Sparrowhawk
- White-tailed eagle
- Golden eagle

Pandionidae
- Osprey

Read on for additional information about these.

Falconidae (falcons)
'Falcon' comes from the Latin word *falcis*, meaning 'sickle'. This describes the wings of these birds: sharp and tapered shapes that make them the speediest birds of prey. The agility that these wings provide allows these birds to change direction seamlessly in

flight. So specialised are these wings that juvenile falcons have longer flight feathers for the first year of their life – to make flying easier while they are still learning – rather like stabilisers on a bicycle.

Falcons kill with their beaks, which have a 'tooth' on the side that helps with this. Hawks and eagles, on the other hand, kill with their feet.

As with the other birds of prey, falcons have fantastic eyesight – up to 2.6 times that of an average human. Their large, dark eyes are generally more appealing to humans than the intense, stark eyes of kites, hawks, eagles and osprey. Perhaps these eyes remind us of open, dilated pupils – subconsciously linking to connection and attraction. These big eyes, along with these birds' smaller size, make falcons seem 'cuter' and 'sweeter' than other birds of prey.

Falcons nest in scrapes or squats.

Accipitridae (kites, hawks and eagles) and *Pandionidae* (osprey)

These birds glide on broad wings that have discernible 'fingers' at their ends. Although powerful, these wings are not as streamlined, and as a consequence these birds aren't as fast or agile as falcons, or as capable of long chases. Therefore these birds are just as likely to swoop from a perch as to dive through the sky for prey.

The majority have white, yellow or orange eyes with large black pupils that make them appear more dangerous-looking than falcons. In the case of the goshawk and sparrowhawk, these eyes match their fierce, killing instinct – something we humans find fascinating and unnerving in equal measure.

Accipitridae comes from the Latin word *accipere*, meaning 'to grasp' – probably referring to the long, sharp talons that these birds use to catch and kill their victims. The term 'hawk' is frequently used to describe birds of prey that live in wooded areas.

The osprey is the solitary member of the *Pandionidae* family, as a unique, fish-hunting specialist.

Many of these bird species are builders of proper – and often epic – nests.

Overarching facts

Size

As you go through this book, you will discover that in certain cases, the male and female do not look the same. This is called sexual dimorphism. Also, the female is normally larger than the male, and this is called reversed sexual size dimorphism.

Feathers

Feathers are understandably very important to birds of prey: the quality of them is essential. When a bird experiences trauma or a lack of food while its feathers are growing, this appears on its feathers as 'stress' or 'fret' marks: pale lines across the feather.

Each pale line is a weakness; the feather is vulnerable to breaking across these points. And each broken feather means less support for surrounding feathers, leading to further breakages. This hinders the bird's ability to fly and hunt effectively, thereby giving it a much lower chance of survival.

Eyesight

Birds of prey's eyes are usually as large as or larger than an adult human's, which is massive in relation to their body size. Where a human has 20,000 photoreceptor cells in their eyes, birds of prey have many more – with a buzzard having one million of these cells. Consequently they can see the world in much greater detail than we can; the images in their binocular-like eyes are magnified by up to 30%.

Prey

Ironically, despite their speed, power and amazing eyesight – and being famed as fantastic hunters – the success rate of birds of prey catching their quarry is surprisingly low: between 5–10% on average. Bird, insect and mammal prey can scarper very quickly!

Furthermore, birds of prey are methodical and predictable in their hunting. They tend to stay loyal to a particular area, hunting there daily for years, meaning that their prey can adapt their habits in response. For example, a small mammal may choose to forage in denser vegetation or in rainy conditions – weather in which birds of prey do not usually hunt. A victim of a successful hunt might be a young, inexperienced creature, a weaker specimen, or one taken completely by surprise.

Each bird of prey has its own hunting technique and style, as you will discover in each chapter.

Birds of prey and humans

Falconry

Even if birds of prey cannot make a catch every time, their skills are still better than ours in this respect. For this reason we have a long history of turning their natural talents to our advantage. In his 1951 book, *The Goshawk*, T.H. White describes falconry as perhaps 'the oldest sport persisting in the world', explaining the existence of a 'bas-relief of a Babylonian with a hawk on his fist', dating from over 3,000 years ago.

It is believed that falconry came to Europe around AD 400, following invasion by the Huns and Alans from the east. In the twelfth century, the pursuit was integral to Norman culture. When carried out on foot, it was called 'hawking', on horseback, 'falconry'.

The longevity of falconry is due to its use for our sustenance as well as sport: a well-trained bird of prey was a vital tool for catching wild animals that we could eat. For nobles and royalty, conversely, it was a pastime for fun and showing status. (Lower classes may have enjoyed it as a sport too, but there is – as can be expected – less written evidence to support this.)

In early English falconry texts, the male falcon or hawk was referred to as a 'tiercel' or 'tercel', since he is often around a third smaller than the female. The female hawk was called a 'hawk', while 'falcon' referred to the female peregrine falcon.

Flying Turbo the kestrel at Huxley's Bird of Prey Centre. (Photo kindly taken by Claudia Harflett)

In *The Book of St Albans* (generally attributed to Dame Juliana Berners and printed in 1486), a hierarchy of birds of prey was set out according to the social ranks each bird was deemed appropriate for:

- Emperor: eagle and merlin
- Prince: falcon gentles
- Earl: peregrine falcon
- Young man: hobby
- Yeoman: goshawk
- Poor man: tercel
- Priest: sparrowhawk
- Knave or servant: kestrel

Falconry was at its most popular in the UK during the seventeenth century. It fell out of fashion during the eighteenth and early nineteenth centuries when firearms became the main tool used for hunting. A number of falconry books were published in the late nineteenth and early twentieth centuries, however, creating a brief revival.

In his book, T.H. White describes birds of prey as falling into two categories: 'long-winged hawks' (falcons including hobbies and kestrels), whose first primary feather is the longest, and 'short-winged hawks' (such as goshawks, buzzards and eagles), whose fourth primary feather is the longest.

A keeper of a long-winged hawk was a falconer, while that of a short-winged hawk was an austringer.

Nowadays the term falconry is used as a catch-all term for the training of any bird of prey.

Inventions, connections and inspiration

Interesting cultural connections and ways in which our birds of prey have influenced us are scattered throughout the chapters of this book. But it is worth mentioning here that, unsurprisingly, aeroplanes are based on the streamlined shapes of birds. That's why many have been named after them, like the Harrier jump jet – a plane that takes off vertically from the ground, just like the hen harrier and marsh harrier can.

Persecution

This book relays the fact that our birds of prey are still persecuted and killed by humans. This is illegal and a crime. If you come across a dead or injured bird, in what looks like suspicious circumstances, please call the police on 101 or 999. Crimes in progress can be reported online here: www.rspb.org.uk/birds-and-wildlife/advice/wild-bird-crime-report-form

Find out how to recognise and report wild bird crimes here: www.rspb.org.uk/birds-and-wildlife/advice/how-to-report-crimes

Birdwatching

As you learn about our birds of prey, and become familiar with their habits and the environments they live in, you will have a better chance of spotting one for yourself. Then over time, and with practise, this skill of yours will develop and refine.

The best start is to go to the correct type of habitat and look around, keeping an eye out for features such as boulders, trees or other positions that the bird might use as a lookout spot. Scan the skies for its silhouette (you can get illustrated guides to help you with this) and look for signs on the ground: droppings, plucked feathers and carcasses can be a telltale sign of a bird of prey living in the area.

Ethics

While it is an incredibly enjoyable pastime to view and admire birds of prey in the wild (after all, this is probably why you purchased or were gifted this book), we must remember to do this ethically. They do not exist for our entertainment; hence we should treat them and their environment with respect.

Birds of prey are vulnerable to disturbance. For that reason, please keep your distance and do not interfere with the nest. If you get too close, adults may abandon the nest and their eggs/chicks. If the bird flies away, makes repeated alarm calls or appears distressed in any way, you're too close and should move on. Remember that these birds and their nests are protected by law.

One tip is to use camouflage to blend into the background, thus lowering the chance of disturbance. Go into a hide if there is one. Be still and quiet. It makes for a much better experience for you and the bird. You may also grant yourself a longer time to observe it by doing so. Binoculars and scopes can give you good views from a distance.

Don't play recordings of bird calls to encourage the bird to respond or react – you could be diverting it from important duties, especially during the breeding season. This is another form of disturbance.

It goes without saying that you should take any litter away with you. Please try to stick to established paths and roads, and also be careful where you tread. These environments are home to other wildlife and plants as well. Aim for as little human impact as possible.

Eco-tourism

There are undoubtedly many positive aspects of eco-tourism, including the contribution to local economies and the raising of awareness of conservation issues.

However, we should be careful not to over-saturate an area – especially a wild one – with our presence. This is something that we will need to address over the coming years, to prevent wildlife disturbance and damage being done to these precious environments.

With my book, I want people to learn and fuel their passion for nature. I want them to connect with birds of prey and have amazing experiences that they will treasure forever. But I don't want them to contribute to the myriad problems that our wildlife and landscapes already face, so please be mindful.

Watching a white-tailed eagle through a scope. (© Rose Newbold)

THE SECRET LIFE OF BIRDS OF PREY

CHAPTER 1

Peregrine falcon

Scientific name	*Falco peregrinus*
Family	*Falconidae* (falcons)
UK conservation status	Green

History and current situation

A strong, powerful and inspiring bird of prey, the peregrine falcon was revered by many ancient cultures. In Egyptian mythology, the god Horus had the head of a falcon, and was both a sun and falcon god. The eye of Horus – a human eye with the plumage pattern of a falcon's cheek – was a symbol used to heal and protect against

Flying peregrine falcon with prey. (@ Graham Parkinson)

Female peregrine falcon on nest box at St Albans Cathedral. (© Patrick Wainwright; see story on page 26)

evil. Indigenous Americans believed the bird to be a messenger who brought guidance from the spirit world. In Celtic folklore, the sight of a peregrine falcon was believed to be a warning to be careful and to keep your eyes open for dangers.

During the Middle Ages, kings and nobles utilised the peregrine falcon to hunt for sport, and the bird was protected by royal decree. Its good temperament made the bird easy to train. The saying 'a bird in the hand is worth two in the bush' came about to describe how one trained falcon was more valuable to man than two wild ones.

Naturalist Albertus Magnus of Cologne gave the peregrine its scientific name, referring to its habit of peregrinating (wandering) to follow its food sources out of the area when not in the breeding season.

In 1940, the government issued a 'Destruction of Peregrine Falcon Order', which resulted in the killing of around 600 birds, with eggs and nests taken and destroyed. This was done as peregrine falcons were seen as interfering with homing pigeons released by crashed airmen during the Second World War.

Peregrine numbers were particularly low during the 1950s and 1960s due to pesticides in the food chain and human persecution. Toxic agricultural chemicals such as Dichlorodiphenyltrichloroethane (DDT) built up to high levels in peregrines, whose diet consists of a lot of seed-eating birds. This resulted in adult mortality, eggshell thinning and less successful breeding. By 1964, only 20% of the UK population had survived, with only those living in remote Scottish Highlands unaffected.

The banning of certain chemicals and the introduction of protective legislation (the Wildlife and Countryside Act 1981) led to a slow recovery in the bird's numbers, which had almost returned to pre-decline levels by the late 1990s.

And yet the peregrine falcon is still illegally killed by humans who fear the predation of their game birds or racing pigeons. The Scottish Raptor Study Group estimates that a quarter of all peregrine nests in south and east Scotland are victims of interference or killing. In addition, peregrine eggs and chicks are sometimes stolen for collections or falconry purposes.

While targeted action to help peregrines is challenging, conservation charities are assisting them with the provision of nesting ledges and boxes, in particular to encourage the recolonisation of their previous ranges in south and east England.

Peregrines have also managed to expand their range into urban environments, with peregrine falcon nests on buildings becoming common across the UK. Examples include Norwich Cathedral and, in 2022, a pair bred on St Albans Cathedral for the first time.

Office workers might spot peregrine falcons swooping between the skyscrapers in mega cities such as London and Manchester. These tall buildings mimic clifftop locations and the urban microclimate provides the birds with warmth and shelter, as well as an abundance of pigeons that make up the majority of their diet!

There are now an estimated 1,500 peregrine breeding pairs in the UK.

Description, characteristics and behaviour

The peregrine falcon's feathers are blue-grey in colour, except on its white chin and chest (the latter of which is finely barred with grey or black). It also sports a striking black 'moustache'. These darker feathers are known as a malar stripe, which reduces the effect of the sun's glare into the bird's eyes, which is particularly useful when it is hunting.

Its legs are yellow, as is the nostril part of its short, hooked beak and the rim around its eyes. Its wings are pointed, long and broad, and its tail is fairly short.

It is a fairly large bird at 39–50cm in length, with a wingspan of 95–115cm. It weighs in at 600–1,300g, with the female being the biggest and heaviest of the two. The peregrine falcon is the largest species of the falcon family in the UK.

The male and female look incredibly similar in terms of their colour and patterning. It is easiest to tell the two apart when they are together: as well as being significantly larger, the female is muscular with a thicker neck, while the male is sleek and streamlined in shape. If you can look closely at details, you may notice that

Female and male peregrine falcons eating a pigeon. (© Dave Newbold)

the female is more heavily marked than the male, and has vertical stripes around her throat, which he does not have. Further to this, the male's white plumage is a lot brighter than the female's, which is off-white with a tinge of beige or pink. Juvenile peregrines' feathers are browner and darker.

The peregrine falcon's most common prey is medium-sized birds. Its main hunting technique is to spot its prey, tuck in its wings and straighten its tail, before diving steeply at great speed to catch it. This dive is known as a stoop. This bird is able to reach over 200mph in a stoop (faster than the world's speediest roller coaster), making it the fastest animal on earth.

Naturally, the peregrine's features have evolved to withstand flying at this speed. One of these features is its nostrils, within which scientists have found small protruding cones that allow the bird to breathe at speed. This inspired the design of the first jet engines, which included similar cones so that air could pass into the engines at greater speeds without them choking out.

The peregrine falcon strikes its victim with a ferocious blow from its foot and hind claw to catch it. Unlike other birds of prey that use their feet to kill, falcons such as peregrine falcons deliver fatal stabs with their beaks.

On occasions when it can surprise its prey, the peregrine attacks at lower speeds from the ground or a perch. Although pigeons are their favourite food source, peregrines will eat birds as small as goldcrests. Being larger than the male, the female

THE SECRET LIFE OF BIRDS OF PREY

catches the largest prey. In certain instances, peregrines have been seen taking small mammals, large insects, lizards and amphibians.

The peregrine consumes nearly all of its catch – it only leaves the breastbone, feathered wings and intestines uneaten. It has a special tooth on the side of its beak that helps to tear into its meal.

The adult peregrine is fairly free from predators, except in places where there are eagles. Juveniles and eggs, however, are vulnerable to predation by other peregrines.

Peregrines usually live for five to six years, although one was once recorded at over 16 years old.

Its most common call is a chattering *kek-kek-kek* or *kak-kak-kak-kak*.

Habitat, nesting habits and breeding

As well as urban environments, peregrine falcons can live in marine/intertidal and wetland areas, and on farmland, grassland and uplands. One non-negotiable requirement for peregrine falcons is open areas for hunting in, with suitable prey available.

During the breeding season, the male enacts various moves to solidify his bond with the female before mating. This includes bowing to her, keeping his head low and lifting his tail; doing the same from the nest and calling to her; and giving food to her

St Albans Cathedral's peregrine pair mating. (© Patrick Wainwright; see story on page 26)

on a perch or in mid-air. The latter may be preceded by a display of dynamic aerial acrobatics, with precise spirals and steep dives. The female for her part flies upside down to receive the food from the male's talons.

Peregrine falcon nest sites – which are sited on cliff edges, quarry faces or urban buildings – are called eyries, just like those of eagles. They, unlike most other birds of prey, rarely nest in trees. And they do not build a nest using materials they have brought in. Instead, the female creates a slight scrape using her chest and legs, or just lays her eggs on old debris left on the ledge.

In late March or early April, the female lays up to four eggs at two- to three-day intervals. The eggs are a rich orangey brown or reddish brown (or occasionally a buff or creamy white), with dark brown or almost black markings in the form of speckles, spots or mottles. The parents share incubation duties, unlike many other birds of prey, where this duty falls mainly to the female. This begins after the last or penultimate egg has been laid and lasts for around a month per egg.

After this point, the eggs hatch over a couple of days, with the young being much closer in size to each other than in most other bird of prey species. Peregrines then revert to traditional roles for a couple of weeks, with the female brooding and the male supplying food. The female then shares the task of hunting with the male.

Peregrine chicks are ready to fledge 35–42 days after they hatch. Post fledging, they will be taught how to hunt and handle prey in flight by their parents. After two months or so, they are ready to be independent.

Most individuals remain within 100km of their birthplace. Sadly, only a third of peregrine falcons live to breeding age.

Peregrine falcons are resident birds in the UK. This means they do not migrate to other countries. However, those living in upland environments move to lower ground or the coast in winter. During this time the UK population is joined by individuals migrating from Scandinavia.

Peregrines on the cathedral

Written by St Albans photographer Steve Shand.

My story with St Albans' peregrine falcons goes back to the Covid lockdown period. Back then, I would take dawn walks around the park and lakes so early that I avoided most people apart from the earliest-rising dog walkers and joggers.

It was a time of uncertainty but also peace. I didn't have any work at the time and despite the ever-growing money and pandemic stresses, I found calm on those walks as the sun slowly rose and mist coated the water. Peace, that is, until I found a peregrine on the cathedral. After this my slow, easy feeling was replaced by adrenaline.

THE SECRET LIFE OF BIRDS OF PREY

Young peregrine falcon flying. (© Steve Shand)

On my first encounter, the bird was on the tower, hunched beside brickwork and tucked out of the wind. While I watched it preening and looking out for threats, it was hard to believe this fluffy, unassuming little shape could be a master of the skies.

Of course, I then saw the speed and manoeuvring of it in flight. I was totally unprepared for the way it moved – it was hard to track and pan with my camera's large lens. Every shot was hard-earned. There was minimal warning in the bird's body language as to when it would take flight: a small shake of the feathers and a little head bobbing, then off it went.

Prior to the cathedral, I had only ever seen peregrine falcons on a rocky coastline in Scotland at high speed and by chance. After I first watched that bird fly that exciting morning, I returned again and again to the cathedral. However, whether it was my timing or the bird actually being absent, sometimes it would seem to disappear for a few months. I was either missing the bird or it was away on 'other' business.

What I would never have thought at the time was that the following spring, the cathedral would come alive to the sound of what I would assume was that same bird,

Peregrine with great spotted woodpecker. (© Steve Shand)

older now and with adult plumage. The year before it retained some of the brown tones of youth (see photo on page 27), but now it was a proud grey and white bird accented with black.

Furthermore, it wasn't alone. It had a partner. And what a partner! Both birds were strong and magnificent. I couldn't wait to see whether what I hoped might happen would.

Over the spring months the pair worked hard to establish and protect their territory and to make their home on the cathedral. I and all the other local nature lovers and photographers waited with baited breath.

Our patience was rewarded when, to our delight, a chick was hatched successfully! This was when the pair's work really began. Feeding their offspring seemed a never-ending task, and the shrill calls of the parents echoed off the brick walls while new prey items were brought in over and over. A pigeon, a blackbird, a great spotted woodpecker – the falcons were indiscriminate. Whatever it took to feed their chick, and at any cost, they would do it.

I was amazed by the parents' dedication and persistence. One time I watched the male take off and make a pretend casual flight around the spire of the cathedral, just to come back and stoop towards the pigeons on the grass below, which were a little too comfortable – possibly unaware of the threat above or just too used to the falcons' presence.

THE SECRET LIFE OF BIRDS OF PREY

As time went on, the chick was growing out of sight from most people's eyes. I know from those that were keeping tabs on the chick that she was growing at an alarming pace. Nature needs to move quickly!

Despite return visits I never actually saw the juvenile myself. Although that may sound disappointing, nature sometimes has a way of keeping its secrets and that's just how it is. As a human you are privileged to gain a little insight or glimpse from time to time, and these treasured moments stay in your mind forever.

From the photos I have seen, the juvenile was perfect and beautiful. Yet although the little one seemed capable and strong, it's a big world out there. I wish her the best of luck in finding her way.

More information from Chloé

In 2022, St Albans Cathedral posted updates about the peregrine falcon family's progress on their social media channels. The male peregrine was named Alban and the female Boudica, to honour important figures in the town's history. Alban and Boudica are one of only five pairs of peregrine falcons breeding in Hertfordshire.

Local nature enthusiasts followed the story with anticipation as it was the first peregrine falcon breeding pair to roost on the cathedral. To help the pair along, licensed bird-ringer Barry Trevis constructed and installed a nesting tray on behalf of the Wilder St Albans project: a collaboration between St Albans City and District Council and the Herts and Middlesex Wildlife Trust.

Eventually we learned that two brown eggs had been laid in the box, but would they hatch?

Only one egg actually hatched, on 16/17 May 2022. After announcing the chick's arrival, the cathedral launched a public vote to name her. She was ultimately given the lovely name of Artemis, after the Greek goddess of wild animals and the hunt.

When Artemis was 23 days old, she was ringed by Barry Trevis, with assistance from Steven Moore. At this point she weighed a healthy 950g. She was ringed so that she can be identified in the future, to provide information on her dispersal, movements and survival.

After losing her downy feathers and developing flight feathers over the following fortnight, Artemis fledged around 26 June, and we started to see her learning how to hunt for herself! Her parents taught her the art of grabbing prey in mid-air by dropping food items for her to catch.

Alban and Boudica are likely to return to the cathedral each year to breed together, as peregrine falcons tend to pair for life and stay loyal to their chosen nest site. Therefore we will potentially witness the annual raising of a chick or two at the cathedral, plus we can feel hopeful that peregrine falcons will become a familiar sight across Hertfordshire as young birds like Artemis establish their own territories and nests, and begin to breed themselves.

Artemis after being ringed, with unhatched egg behind her. (© Barry Trevis)

Artemis after fledging. (@ Andrew Steele)

Where to see them

Peregrine falcons may be widespread across the UK, but they remain a comparatively rare bird of prey. They are found in low densities in a few isolated spots in the south and south-east of England, although they are slowly increasing their range. They are found in much higher densities in the upland areas of north-west England, Wales and southern Scotland.

In winter, peregrines from upland environments move to lower ground or the coast, with some heading over to Ireland. During this time they are joined by individuals migrating from Scandinavia. One great place to see them is at east coast marshlands or estuaries, where they hunt. Rainham Marshes in Essex is a top spot.

Peregrine falcons can be found roosting on cathedrals in cities such as Norwich and St Albans, as well as in their traditional clifftop places such as Malham Cove in Yorkshire.

One great way to view these amazing birds is via webcams set up by charities, and through RSPB's 'Date with Nature' events across the UK.

CHAPTER 2

Kestrel

Scientific name	*Falco tinnunculus*
Family	*Falconidae* (falcons)
UK conservation status	Amber

'High there, how he rung upon the rein of a wimpling
wing/In his ecstasy!'

The Windhover by Gerald Manley Hopkins

History and current situation

'Kestrel' comes from the Old French word *crécelle*, meaning rattle, probably referring to the bird's call. Although usually quiet, the kestrel emits an excited, high-pitched *klee-klee-klee* or *kee-kee-kee* cry while mating or feeding its young. The bird's scientific name *tinnunculus* derives from the Latin *tinnulus*, meaning 'shrill' – again based on the bird's call.

Old English names for the bird included *Stannel* (Stone-Yeller), which originates from the bird's habit of perching on stones and boulders rather than in trees on the Yorkshire moors, and nesting on rocky outcrops and cliff edges, from which it might make its call. Another was *Mushafoc* – Mouse Falcon or Moosie Hawk – based on one of its main prey items.

The Old French name eclipsed the Old English ones, to give us the common name of kestrel – most likely due to the dominant use of French terms in falconry. The kestrel (the male of which was called a tercel) was used in falconry as it had the most powerful feet for its size. However, falconers found that it wasn't a bird particularly motivated to hunt, unlike the goshawk and merlin. (Read more about falconry on pages 16–18.)

In the late nineteenth and early twentieth centuries, the kestrel was heavily persecuted, just like most other birds of prey. Gamekeepers were common perpetrators,

Male kestrel. (© Sue Slater)

even though in reality kestrels very rarely took game chicks. During the Second World War kestrels were generally left alone and their numbers recovered.

DDT and similar agricultural chemicals then caused a serious decline in the late 1950s and 1960s, especially in eastern England. Meanwhile, in the coastal areas of the west and south-west, the kestrel remained fairly common as its prey in these areas hadn't been as affected by these chemicals.

Once these chemicals were banned, the kestrel population recovered once more until the 1980s, when it began to decline again. Ever since, kestrel numbers have fluctuated.

It is now believed that over 80% of the UK's kestrel population has disappeared over the last 25 years. The changes in farming systems, including the removal of hedges and the loss of field margins and meadows, means reduced habitat for the kestrel's food sources. The continued use of certain pesticides is another factor. According to the Scottish Raptor Study Group, Scottish vole numbers are decreasing, which would significantly impact kestrel populations.

Currently there are an estimated 46,000 kestrel pairs in the UK. It is one of our most widespread birds of prey, since it can live and hunt in a wide range of environments. Yet, due to its massive decline nationally, we need to protect and conserve the kestrel. One way is to provide nest boxes, as the bird does not build its own nests. These need to be affixed at least 15ft high to isolated trees, poles or buildings in undisturbed locations that are close to grassland and have good visibility.

Description, characteristics and behaviour

At just 32–35cm in length, with a wingspan of 71–80cm and a weight of 156–252g, the kestrel is one of the smallest birds of prey, with only the hobby and merlin being smaller.

Kestrels have chestnut brown backs and upper wings spotted with black, with black flight feathers at the ends of their pointed wings.

The male has a pigeon-grey head, rump and tail, and the end of his long tail has a broad band of black, with a white patch at the tip.

Female kestrel. (© Chloé Valerie Harmsworth)

'Hovering' male kestrel. (© Graham Parkinson)

The female and juvenile have the same chestnut colouring as the male but duller, and instead of the grey parts described above, they are brown. Juvenile males take up to three years to fully acquire their adult plumage, so varying levels of grey can be seen during this time of development.

Both sexes have a creamy buff chest that is streaked with dark vertical lines. Their legs are orange or yellow and their short and chunky hooked beaks are yellow and black in colour.

The kestrel is best known for its habit of hovering over farmland and roadside verges, its wings flapping rapidly and tail fanned out for balance. This has given it the name Windhover in south and west England, or Stand-Gale, and *Cudyll y Gwynt* (Wind Hawk) in Wales.

Technically, it isn't actually hovering. Instead, the kestrel is flying slightly forward, with the wind pushing it back and its neck stretched out to compensate for the force of the wind. It is finding the perfect balance between its own flight and the opposing wind. When the wind speed is high, the kestrel glides; when the wind speed is low, the kestrel flaps to maintain its place.

As the bird does this, its head stays almost completely still – never moving more than 6mm from its position – made possible through the minute adjustments of its wings and tail. This is a technique that requires skill, excellent co-ordination and precision. It is commonly seen hovering above open countryside and over the wildlife-filled verges beside motorways (which is why it is known by some as the Motorway Hawk).

At this elevated vantage point, the kestrel picks out its prey on the ground using its fantastic eyesight. Target chosen, it dives to grab the prey with an extended foot.

Although it is possible for a kestrel to hover on windless days, it would need to constantly flap its wings to keep itself up, and this uses a lot of energy. In these conditions it may employ another hunting method, for example perching on telephone posts, wires or high branches, and looking out for its prey. Another option is to steal the food of other birds, such as that of a short-eared owl, by dive-bombing it until it drops its catch. These methods are particularly useful in winter, when it is vital that the kestrel conserves its energy.

Voles are the kestrel's main source of food; the number of kestrels is closely linked to the number of voles. A good vole year results in a high population of kestrels, and a bad vole year is a terrible one for kestrels. For example, the drought of 1976 hit vole populations hard, and therefore was a difficult year for kestrels too. A kestrel needs to eat four to eight voles a day, depending on the energy it has expended and the time of year. It will catch multiple voles in succession, caching some to consume later the same day, before dusk.

On top of its telescopic eyesight, which allows the kestrel to detect small creatures from a great height, the bird's eyes have adapted to see ultraviolet light. This is bad news for voles, which leave trails of urine that reflect ultraviolet light. This makes it much easier for the kestrel to track them down.

The kestrel also eats other small mammals like shrews, moles, woodmice and sometimes even young rabbits, as well as earthworms, slugs and insects (for example cockchafers, grasshoppers and dung beetles). It also eats the occasional lizard.

The kestrel's sharp eyesight means that it can detect a beetle from 50 metres away – surely inspiring the saying, 'eyes like a hawk'? Once nabbed, small creatures like these are often taken to a nearby fencepost to be consumed.

The kestrel provides a good service to farmers in keeping the number of small rodents and other mammals, who eat the farmers' crops, at a manageable level. (In Yorkshire and Orkney they have been given the name of Mouse Hawk and Mouse Falcon for this reason.) One technique that the kestrel has learned is to follow farm machinery, as they flush out potential prey for them.

Winter is a difficult time for the kestrel as food stocks are lower. Furthermore, if snow covers the ground, mice and voles are hidden from sight – moving under its protective layer – and their trails are too.

The kestrel will also eat small birds. Victims tend to be ground-feeding birds, such as finches and sparrows, caught as they feed or rise from the ground. In winter, the kestrel can benefit from the rise in starling numbers, when our resident birds are joined by those from mainland Europe.

Male kestrel eating. (© Sue Slater)

Small birds are particularly important to the kestrel in town locations, where the availability of small mammals is lower. Rather than taking the small birds they have caught to a perch, the kestrel may pluck these on the ground.

Habitat, nesting habits and breeding

Although the countryside is the ideal habitat for the kestrel, it has adapted to man-made environments and can live in the centre of cities.

Kestrels are largely monogamous and pair for life. Although they separate during winter, a pair will reunite around February time to re-establish their territory and begin breeding activities. They reconnect by circling and chasing each other high into the sky, calling to one another. The male may mock-attack the female repeatedly in flight or while she is perched. They might play with objects together as well. The male then shows the female around potential sites – usually in an area where they have nested before.

Kestrels can breed in their first year; however, they don't tend to do this until their second year.

Kestrels are very tolerant of other pairs, defending just a small area around the nest. Their home range is anywhere from 1–10 square kilometres, depending on the number of other kestrels and food availability in the area.

Not builders of nests, kestrels reuse old nests made by other birds, such as crows or magpies, or ledges on buildings and cliffs. They can happily use nest boxes or holes in trees. Some pairs use their chosen nest for successive years.

In late April or early May, the female lays three to six eggs at two-day intervals. The eggs are whitish and heavily marked with red-brown blotches. She begins to incubate once she has laid the third egg, and will do so for 27–29 days per egg.

The eggs hatch over a period of a few days and the chicks are brooded constantly for the first 14 days until they can control their own body temperature. The male's role is to supply the female and chicks with food throughout the nesting period; the female only hunts if food supplies are low. Once the chicks have reached a good size, she can begin to hunt close by.

Indigestible food, including the bones of mammals, are brought back up and ejected from the throats of the chicks as pellets. These pellets accumulate in the nest, making for a very stinky and flea-ridden environment! The chicks are vulnerable to predation from birds like magpies and crows, as well as other birds of prey.

At four weeks, the chicks begin to fledge. As with many other birds of prey, they explore areas further and further from the nest over time, returning to it to roost for a couple more weeks. They are fed by their parents for around a month after they have fledged, until they have learned to catch their own food. Unlike most other birds

Kestrel chicks in Hertfordshire, showing growth in 12 days. (© Andrew Steele)

of prey, however, kestrel chicks are very friendly with one another and often stay together for a while after fledging.

Only around 20% of kestrels survive two years to reach breeding age. They may then live to around four and a half years; they very rarely make it to their teens. And yet, one was once recorded at 15 years and 11 months old.

Death is usually caused by starvation (especially during winter), with persecution (shooting and poisoning), disease, accidents and collisions being the other causes. They can also be predated by other birds of prey such as goshawks, peregrine falcons and sparrowhawks.

Kestrels are UK residents and do not migrate. However, in autumn, kestrels can adjust their territory according to food supply. If there are a lot of voles in their habitat, they may not need to move; if there aren't many, they will move to an area with a better supply.

Some juveniles move further south at this time, while others might stay within a few miles of their home during their first winter.

Kestrels in the uplands are particularly likely to move south in autumn to areas where temperatures are milder. Where there is less snow, food is easier to find.

During this time they defend their territories, although they will sometimes allow these to overlap.

The Knettishall kestrel

Written by award-winning wildlife blogger and animal rights campaigner Kate Stephenson, from Norwich.

Pushing a buggy trailed by two restless toddlers is perhaps not the easiest way to experience heathland, but it has certainly become the most common way for me to now spend my weekend walks in nature.

Today the air is fresh with the smell of summer grass and the sweet coconutty top notes of factor 50 sun cream. A wasp or two buzz a little too close for comfort, trying their luck with small and sticky ice cream fingers that have yet to be reached and scrupulously cleaned by me.

Across the patchwork texture of gorse, heather and sandy dirt pathways, the summer sun beats down. We push on as wheels bump over the dry track, and child-sized feet drag behind. We don't dare to have any expectations, lest they be shattered.

Away from the dangers of sharp twigs and stinging nettles, my two young children wander freely, stopping now and then to express the shrill excitement of discovering a grasshopper, or to retrieve a particularly handsome stone.

This area of Suffolk, known as Knettishall Heath, is managed by the Suffolk Wildlife Trust as a nature reserve, and its rich biodiversity has seen it designated as a

Male kestrel on a branch. (© Graham Parkinson)

Site of Special Scientific Interest (SSSI). Since my childhood I've visited on occasion, to seek out the many butterflies and moths that float across the heather, or to spot various bird species as they perch, exposed on the tops of small trees and shrubs, which stand scattered like islands in the open, grassy terrain.

As the bright sunshine continues to taunt my lack of sunglasses, a flicker of copper brown catches the corner of my eye as my eldest child exclaims, 'There!' with a pointed finger – as if to respond to the split-second question as it flashes across my mind.

I'm frequently impressed by her keen eye and lightning-speed reaction time. My daughter's interest in the natural world has been well-nurtured at this young age, thanks in particular to the gifts of time and focus that Covid lockdowns have bestowed on us for much of her young life.

I try my best to follow the direction of her pointing, as the sun's rays leave me squinting. Shielding my gaze with my hand, I search the glare of the heathland's open landscape and, fortunately, the brown shape circles back round. This time I have it in my sights before it swiftly passes by again: a kestrel.

Instinctively, we all fall quiet as the impressive bird lands among the top branches of the only tree that stands in the centre of the heath. Even my youngest has lifted his head from the ground-dwelling ants and beetles to join us in our curiosity.

The kestrel sits as still as a statue, watching everything from its vantage point. It's thought that a kestrel's eyesight is up to eight times more powerful than a human's – not only can they spot the movements of a mouse from 200ft away, but they can accurately judge its size, shape and position too.

For only a second or two the bird scans. Possessing the capability to see ultraviolet light invisible to the human eye, it uses this super power to detect the urine trails left by rodents on the ground to locate its prey.

In one swift motion, it lifts into the air, rising above the landscape as an actor on strings might use theatre trickery to impress an audience. In our kestrel's case, the audience is suitably impressed.

With beating wings that rise and fall quickly and steadily, and outstretched like sails, the floating bird shifts its tail from side to side, seemingly using it to secure the perfect point of balance.

Moments pass in silence as the kestrel's speckled body and grey head remain firmly fixed in place, hovering high above us – before it drops like a bungee jumper, free-falling towards the earth. Fast and agile, the bird swoops along the ground, before ascending upwards almost as quickly. Somehow it seems feasible to assume it caught whatever small creature it had in its view.

'Eagle,' my 2-year-old son observes – and it's not too unreasonable to see how he reached such a conclusion.

A hunting female kestrel. (© Dave Newbold)

'Kestrel,' I gently correct. The bird disappears following the same route it circled in on.

'Kestrel,' My daughter repeats, pausing in thought for a second. 'Why is it a kestrel?'

It would seem that 'why' questions make up the majority of her vocabulary of late, and as usual, I'm flummoxed as to how to respond.

'That's just what we call that type of bird, which hovers like that. You sometimes see them hovering in the air at the side of the road when we're driving.'

That seems enough to satisfy, and together we continue slowly on our mini expedition.

Where to see them

Kestrels are found year round in most counties in the UK. RSPB Rye Meads in Hertfordshire is one good place to see them.

The best environment in which to spot kestrels is on farmland, heathland and grassland, and in urban environments that have adjacent open spaces for hunting. Kestrels can also be found on rugged coastland and hills. Places where they can nest, such as in trees, on crags or on high buildings, must be nearby.

In autumn, some kestrels from the uplands move south.

Keep a (careful) eye out for them hovering above verges when you are driving on a motorway.

You are unlikely to see kestrels in treeless wetlands or dense forests.

The direct flight of a travelling kestrel, high in the sky, can be mistaken for a peregrine falcon.

Kestrel direct flight. (© Barry Madden)

CHAPTER 3

Merlin

Scientific name	*Falco columbarius*
Family	*Falconidae* (falcons)
UK conservation status	Red

History and current situation

The word 'Merlin' is derived from the French *émerillon*, which comes from the Latin *merula*, meaning blackbird. This is the largest prey that the merlin was believed to take; in the same way that the goshawk is named after the goose. Conversely, the scientific name of *columbarius* is more ambitious, suggesting the merlin could catch a pigeon or dove, and they are known as pigeon hawks in North America.

Interestingly, the Old French word *ésmerillon* means swivel, which could perhaps relate to the bird's ability to change direction seemingly on a pin in flight.

Due to its diminutive size, the merlin was popular with lady falconers. Indeed, it was classed as the 'the falcon for a lady' in the fifteenth-century *Book of St Albans* (see more about this text on page 18).

In the twentieth century, the merlin was used to hunt larks. In the context of falconry, the male merlin was known as Jack, a word that has been used historically to mean small or fast.

Since the late nineteenth century, merlin numbers have experienced widespread decline, probably as a result of habitat loss through the over-management of moorlands and the removal or burning of the heather they need to nest within, as well as increased disturbance and persecution (particularly by gamekeepers on grouse moors, even though merlins rarely take game birds).

As with other birds of prey, merlins were badly affected by the use of toxic organochlorine pesticides in the 1950s and 1960s. Their population was at an all-time low in 1960 with only 550 pairs left in the UK. It wasn't until the early 1980s that their population started to show signs of recovery, although this was slow and hindered

Young merlin on a branch. (© Graham Parkinson)

by the overgrazing of animals and afforestation that reduced the amount of suitable habitat.

Although the merlin population recovered, with a 94% increase, the bird is on the red list in terms of its conservation status in the UK. This is partly because the merlin is the most heavily contaminated bird of prey in the UK, with northern individuals especially carrying inexplicably high levels of mercury in their systems. This and the other contaminants found within the bird are being monitored in the hopes that this mystery can be solved and something done about it.

Conservation attempts to help merlins are rarely successful due to the low population densities of the bird in any given area. Therefore it is vital that land use policies include specialist provisions and ensure that merlin feeding and nesting requirements are protected, so that numbers do not dwindle once more. For example, heather moorlands, forests and agricultural land need to be managed sympathetically, allowing vegetation needed for nesting to grow, with vigilance against egg hunters and collectors.

There are currently an estimated 900–1,500 breeding merlin pairs in the UK.

Description, characteristics and behaviour

The merlin is the UK's smallest bird of prey at 25–30cm in length, with a wingspan of 50–62cm. In fact, it is not much larger than the blackbird after which it is named.

Being petite, the adult merlin is sometimes preyed on by larger birds of prey, including the peregrine falcon and goshawk. However, the merlin can be fearless and aggressive, which puts a lot of carnivorous birds off!

The female is the largest of the pair at 164–300g, while the male weighs 125–234g. There is less of a stark difference in size between the two when compared to most other birds of prey, which makes it harder to tell them apart from a distance.

The merlin's wings are shorter than those of other falcons, and are broad-based and pointed. Its barred tail is long and square-cut at the end rather than rounded, with a conspicuous dark terminal bar. It flies with rapid wingbeats, or glides at a fast rate, holding its wings close to its body.

The female and juvenile merlin look similar to the hobby, with dark grey/blue or black flecks and stripes on top of the cream on their chest, tail and the underside of their wings.

In the case of the male, however, his chest and the top part of the underside of his wings are suffused with orange – reminiscent of a male sparrowhawk.

The feathers on the top side of the female are shades of brown and those on the top side of the male are blue-grey with darker streaks.

Female merlin at Rainham Marshes. (© Barry Jackson)

Merlin 'mantling' to protect its catch. (© Mark Hunter/Adobe Stock)

Both sexes and the juveniles have yellow legs, a yellow ring around their eye and yellow on the nostril section at the top of their beaks. Their beaks are medium in length, hooked, grey and chunky. The merlin's facial moustache is less defined than on other falcons, such as the hobby. Importantly, the merlin does not sport the hobby's rusty red 'trousers'.

The merlin, as with other falcons, is a fast flier and hunts small birds including meadow pipits and larks. It eats insects such as beetles and moths, as well as small mammals (i.e. rodents) when needed, to help it achieve its requirement of 35–50g of food per day.

Its main hunting technique is to perch at a slightly elevated position, for example on a tree stump or rock (or even on the back of a sheep!), from which vantage it can locate its prey. Once a target has been chosen, the merlin tends to attack using the element of surprise, with a short-distanced, low and fast flight – although it carries out prolonged chases if necessary.

The merlin rarely soars, but when pursuing skylarks, it may utilise warm updrafts of air to achieve the height needed to catch these high-flying songsters. It also sometimes employs the hang-in-the-breeze method to drop onto victims from above, as the kestrel does, as well as the peregrine falcon's vertical stoop.

The merlin's prey is usually caught close to or on the ground after a furious, twisting chase. The success rate of an attack varies depending on the hunting method used and the type of prey the bird has chosen.

The merlin's call is a *ki-ki-ki-ki* or *cheo-cheo-cheo*, and a piercing whistle.

The merlin lives for an average of three years, although the oldest found was almost 13 years old!

Habitat, nesting habits and breeding

Like most other birds of prey, the merlin is adaptable and can live in a variety of habitats: marine and intertidal, wetlands, uplands, grasslands and farmland. Often an inhabitant of stony moorlands, it is also known as the Stone Falcon in Wales and Scotland and as the Rock Falcon, Stone Hawk or Rock Kestrel in the north of England.

Merlins stay loyal to their breeding territory, with both sexes marking their territory with high, circling, soaring displays. A territory is used year after year, and by successive generations, although the exact location of a pair's nest will vary.

To ward off rivals, the male may demonstrate rapid wing beats followed by impressive mid-air rolls. He can also dive, flutter and perform other styles and shapes of flight.

Merlins become sexually mature at one year old. Most female merlins breed at this time, while males tend to wait until their second year. As part of their courtship, the

Merlin in flight. (© Richard/Adobe Stock)

female may crouch on the ground calling loudly, with her tail raised, as the male circles above her. The male may display by flying with rapid wing beats interspersed with glides, while uttering a *kik-kik-kik* call. They copulate once he lands. Courtship is often accompanied by food exchanges.

After mating, the male and female frequently hunt together as a pair. Before bringing food back to the nest, they pluck and decapitate their prey (see photo on page 49).

The UK population of merlin are unique in that they nest on the ground, concealed in deep, old heather (outside the UK, ground-nesting merlins are a rare occurrence). While the majority of our native merlins do this, since the 1970s some have begun to nest in trees that stand at the edge of conifer plantations, particularly in the old nests of corvids or other large birds. This adaptation mirrors the habits of continental merlins, and may help the bird to survive in places where there is little to no heather available.

In the case of the ground nest, the female creates a shallow scrape in the soil and lines this with small twigs, bracken, heather and other material. The ideal nest site has an expansive view of the surrounding moorland and nearby lookout posts.

Between May and early June, the female lays three to five eggs that are buff in colour with red-brown spots, in two-day intervals. Both she and the male incubate the eggs, starting as soon as the last egg has been laid. After being incubated for around a month, the eggs hatch close together.

The female generally remains close to the nest and defends it from intruders and predators, attacking birds many times her size and strength as necessary. Both the adults and their young are susceptible to predation from corvids and other birds of prey. For this reason, merlins will dive-bomb larger birds to drive them away (see photo on page 52).

The male provides food before the eggs are laid, all the way to when the young fledge. The female occasionally hunts once the chicks are ten days old.

Close to the nest will be a post or boulder: the spot where the merlin plucks and prepares food. There will be a collection of discarded feathers and bones here. This is sometimes given as a reason for the other merlin names, for example Stone Falcon, given at the start of this section.

In ground nests, the chicks leave the nest at around 20 days old and scatter into the surrounding undergrowth; however, they do not fully fledge until they are a month old. The reason for this scatter approach is to avoid predation and increase their chances of survival; the parents continue to care for them during this time.

A month after fledging, the young merlins become fully independent. There is a 23% chance that they will survive their first year.

If the pair experiences an early egg loss, they can lay replacement clutches, thus still raising their annual brood.

Merlin with decapitated prey. (© Peter Ryan Outdoors/Adobe Stock)

Our merlins are residents in the UK year round; they do not migrate to other countries in the winter. However, merlins from north European countries and Iceland come to the UK to join them, to make the most of our warmer climate before returning to their breeding countries in April and May.

Merlin magic

Written by writer and photographer Craig Dibb, who currently lives in Orkney.

The merlin was the last of the British falcons to reveal itself to me. I thought, perhaps, I had glimpsed one before, darting over a drystone wall as I drove past on a grey November day, but I can't be sure. It was just a glimpse.

New birds often reveal themselves slowly. In glimpses. A snappy flight across a river clearing. A silhouette circling against a rising sun. A vanishing tail through the undergrowth. Through these short encounters, you slowly paint a picture of the species, piecing the jigsaw puzzle together bit by bit until you can recognise the bird in a heartbeat.

My first sighting of a merlin, one I can incontestably say *was* a merlin, occurred on a windswept day in the midst of an Orcadian winter. The December sun was passing its meridian, skirting the horizon in a low furtive arc. On the west coast of Orkney, the Atlantic was making war with the land. The sea hung in the air, atomised. The light spread strong and golden in the suspended sea mist, which drifted slowly a mile or more inland. All the while, wave after wave came crashing into the cliffsides below.

I was walking with a friend, the coastal path beneath our feet and heading south into the sunlight – the wild ocean to the right and a heather-clothed hill rising to the left. Above the din of the ocean, there was little room for noise, few airwaves spare.

In my periphery, there was a dash of movement, and a snipe, flushed from the heather, came zigzagging down the hillside. Its alarm came from all around, as if echoing from the sea mist itself. From where I had seen the flash on the moor, a

Merlin flying. (© rayhennessy/Adobe Stock)

bird of prey rose into the strong orange light. Its profile was distinct. A rounded head. Hooked bill silhouetted. The wings tapering to a sharp point. With a jolt, that primordial cognition we all have buried so deep came up and said 'falcon'.

The bird appeared brown and was smaller than any falcon I had seen before. Its pace was slow, which I would learn is rare to see in this bird. After the frenzy of its failed attack on the snipe, it rose up and circled twice, coming about into the wind after each turn, before flying deeper into the moor.

In the months following this sighting, the merlin gave me further glimpses. Nothing lasting. Not one for attention seeking, the merlin is fast, usually seen in that thin region inches above the ground, in a high-octane craze as if fuelled by too much coffee. I saw blurs and dashes here and there. From a distance, while driving, I watched a murmuration of starlings rippling like a stone thrown into a still pond. A merlin was repeatedly diving into their midst.

Orkney is known for its birds. The archipelago catches rare passerines, and it has been the main refuge for the hen harrier during its dark years of persecution on mainland Britain. It's also the site of one of the longest-running bird of prey studies, carried out by the ornithologist Eddie Balfour. An RSPB reserve that bears his name sits at the site of this study and it is an excellent place to watch hen harriers courting and breeding.

I visited the hide there in mid-summer and enjoyed the sight of both male and female hen harriers gracefully quartering the moorland and passing food for their young. They floated effortlessly across the hillside, wings outstretched in a shallow 'V'. The male shone silver in the sunlight, the fingers of his wing tips black. He disappeared beyond the ridgeline for long periods of time while the female tended to stay close, her rich brown colours blending in with the heather and only the white button of her rump standing out.

Towards the end of that afternoon, the female hen harrier crossed the hillside, a kill hanging from a single talon. As she passed over the heather, a flash of brown passed my view through my binoculars. The harrier glanced over her shoulder, panic in her posture. Above her was a falcon, diving aggressively, again and again, in steep, sharp stoops.

At that moment, all my glimpses fitted together. The puzzle was complete. I could see instantly that it was a merlin. A female, and ferocious. The hen harrier looked up at her attacker, her graceful flight now ungainly. I could just about hear the aggressive, chattering alarm call of the merlin on the warm afternoon breeze. At the trough of each attacking dive she received, the hen harrier rolled and twisted, tummy up, her yellow talons bright in the sunshine, open in defence.

Finally, the merlin turned and flew back at intense speed, disappearing into the heather from where she had come. She was just defending her territory, leaving the harrier to fly to her own nest. It was quiet once more on the hillside.

These birds are neighbours and this is probably a daily occurrence. For the entire time the merlin had been in view she was a raging ball of energy. She carried intensity as if she could only be off or on, at full capacity, with no in-between.

I left the hide that afternoon itching for my next glimpse.

Where to see them

Merlins can be found all year in England, Scotland, Wales and Ireland. Although they are widespread, they are not commonly seen. The most likely situation in which you will see a merlin is when it is driving a larger bird away from its territory.

Merlin seeing off a threat. (© William/Adobe Stock)

THE SECRET LIFE OF BIRDS OF PREY

If you catch sight of a hunting merlin, it will usually be moving at breakneck speed, slicing through the sky like a miniature missile. It will be moving so fast that you probably won't see it for long! This will be in an open space; the merlin can't pursue its prey through dense woodland like a sparrowhawk can, as it doesn't possess quite the same agility.

In the summer months, merlins are scattered in small numbers across upland moorland from Shetland to south-west England, and in the winter they move south to inland lowlands and the coast. During this time they are joined by merlins from north Europe and Iceland.

Look for them in open countryside, but especially when you are by the coast. Try reedbeds and bogs too, and on heathlands where they live alongside hen harriers.

RSPB reserves that host merlins during the summer include those in Forsinard, Highland, Glenborrodale in Fort William and Trumland (Orkney).

In winter, try Blacktoft Sands in Yorkshire, Martin Mere in Lancashire, Marshside in Merseyside, Dee Estuary in Cheshire, Elmley Marshes in Kent, Pulborough Brooks in Sussex and Ballynahone Nature Reserve in Northern Ireland.

CHAPTER 4

Hobby

Scientific name	*Falco subbuteo*
Family	*Falconidae* (falcons)
UK conservation status	Green

History and current situation

The hobby was another popular bird in falconry, due to its boldness and courage, and it was used to hunt birds such as larks and quails. According to *The Book of St Albans*, the hobby was considered the appropriate hunting bird for a young man.

The etymology of the word 'hobby' comes from the Old French *hober*, meaning 'to stir', which perhaps describes how this bird can stir up roosts and flocks of other birds while hunting.

Interestingly, the inventor Peter Adolph wanted to name the table-top football game he created after his favourite bird: the trademark was not granted for 'hobby', so the bird's species name *subbuteo* was chosen instead.

Subbuteo means 'smaller than the buzzard' – a not-very-useful description in distinguishing the hobby from our other petite birds of prey! Another name given to the hobby is Jack, indicating its small size, as with the merlin.

Over 70% of heathland – the ideal habitat for the hobby – has been lost in south England over the last 200 years. This is the result of agriculture, urban development and afforestation (the planting of trees where there were previously few or none).

On the flip side, it is believed that the hobby suffered much less from pesticide use compared to other birds of prey, due to its diet of insects and birds that eat insects. One exception is that it will eat skylarks, which consume seeds and therefore some of these dangerous toxins would have been passed on.

As the number of reservoirs and flooded gravel pits has increased in recent decades, followed by dragonfly numbers, the hobby population has seen an upward curve.

Hobby. (© Russell Sherriff)

The improved, more widespread availability of its food has meant that the hobby has been able to spread further northwards from its original haunts in south England. The UK's warming climate may be a factor in increasing insect numbers, benefitting the hobby immensely.

Despite this, the hobby is still the victim of persecution from humans, as all birds of prey are.

There are currently around 2,800 hobby breeding pairs in the UK.

Description, characteristics and behaviour

The hobby is similar in size but a bit smaller than the kestrel (one of its closest UK relatives), with an average length of 28–36cm, a wingspan of 70–92cm and weight of 131–340g.

Agile and acrobatic like its other closest UK relatives, the peregrine falcon and merlin, the hobby is reminiscent of a giant swift, with long scythe-like pointed wings and a habit of chasing prey with a fast, dashing flight. It can accelerate and undertake high-speed manoeuvres (when diving and swooping it can achieve nearly 100mph) and sudden changes in direction while doing so.

The top side of the hobby's plumage is a uniform shade of dark greyish brown or almost black, that comes over its head and around its eyes in a helmet, and down each

Hobby underside while in flight.
(© Graham Parkinson)

creamy cheek in a vertical line to form a drooping moustache shape next to its beak. Its face, to me, is reminiscent of the peregrine falcon.

The hobby is darker in colour than the kestrel but has the same sweet, soulful eyes. It has a white eyebrow-stripe that gives it a look of intelligence, and its chin and cheeks are creamy white. Its beak is the classic falcon shape: dark, short, chunky and hooked.

The underside of the hobby's plumage consists of distinctive streaks of white and brown/black down its breast and across the underside of its wings. The deviations from this monotone look include its yellow legs, the yellow ridge on its beak and yellow ring around its eyes, as well as its rusty orange-red thigh feathers and under-tail. Its orange-red 'trousers' are a useful way to distinguish it from the kestrel, the merlin and the (much larger) peregrine falcon.

It can be difficult to tell the male and female hobby apart, as they are similar in look and size!

Juveniles are browner, with no red on their thighs or under their tail.

The hobby flies in a casual manner behind the cover of trees before dashing out suddenly to grab its prey – potentially from a flock of hirundine birds (house martins, sand martins etc.). It is one of the few birds able to catch swallows and swifts in flight. When flying after this prey, the hobby can hold its wings back and fly in a similar way, so that it can get closer before the victim realises it is a predator.

As well as small birds, the hobby hunts bats and insects, such as dragonflies, beetles and moths.

The hobby often catches prey in its talons before transferring the food to its beak while still in the air. With insects, it peels off the outer layer, legs and wings – letting

Hobby reaching for an insect in mid-air. (© Graham Parkinson)

this fall to the ground – before consuming the rest. A hobby can eat up to a dozen insects a minute.

It tends to hunt at the beginning and end of the day, spending the rest of its time resting in a tree. The hobby's large eyes allow it to hunt well into the twilight hours.

The hobby's call is a high-pitched *kyu-kyu-kyu-kyu*.

Adult hobbies do not have any known predators. They live for five years on average, but can live up to ten years. The oldest wild hobby recorded was almost 15 years old.

Habitat, nesting habits and breeding

The hobby is a summer resident in the UK and breeds in all regions of England, as well as southern Scotland (Scotland's first breeding pair was recorded in 2001) and eastern and southern Wales. It has not yet made it to west Wales or north Scotland, and it does not breed in Ireland. However, it is making its way northwards through Scotland.

The hobby can live in a variety of habitats: wetland, farmland, heathland, grassland and woodland. It can survive in both urban and countryside environments. It needs open areas to hunt in.

However, trees and open woodland are vital to the hobby for breeding, which probably led to its other names of Tree Hawk and Tree Falcon. The monogamous pair raise their young in a nest built by another bird – for example a crow's nest.

Juvenile hobby. (© Anton Mir-Mar/Adobe Stock)

The ideal location for a hobby nest is somewhere on the edge of a small woodland or spinney, with nearby access to bodies of water such as wetlands or flooded gravel pits, to source food for growing hobby chicks.

The hobby is very territorial and defensive, particularly when it comes to goshawks and ravens, attacking them to move them on. This helps other birds including pigeons, who happily set up home close to hobby nests to enjoy this protected area.

In June, the female hobby lays two to three eggs that are yellowy buff to reddish tan in colour and mottled all over with reddish to dark brown marks.

After a month of incubation, the hobby eggs hatch. Unlike many other bird species, whose eggs tend to hatch at intervals of two to three days, the hobby's eggs can hatch very close together, on the same or following day.

During the breeding season, the hobby parents mainly feed themselves and their young with small birds rather than insects, as food quantity is crucial during this time. Indeed, the bird times its breeding to sync up with the abundance of young hirundines. Despite its preference for small birds during this season, the hobby also takes advantage of the glut of dragonflies in July to feed its newly hatched chicks.

The hobby chicks are usually ready to fledge following a month of being cared for in the nest.

Juveniles are fully independent by the end of the summer, before the time of migration arrives. Less than half of them survive their first year, but those that do begin to breed at around two years old.

The hobby is the only UK falcon that migrates.

In early autumn (September and October), the hobby migrates (sometimes in small groups) and heads south to tropical Africa, where it spends the winter following rain clouds full of insects.

It returns to our shores in late March/April, having flown thousands of miles.

Hobby pair in flight. (© NickVorobey.com/Adobe Stock)

The sign

A special moment recalled by Anna Gilbert-Falconer, who lives in St Davids in Wales, and works for regenerative ocean farm Câr-Y-Môr and Falcon Boats Wildlife Tours.

My wife Tracey and I live in one of the most beautiful parts of the UK: St Davids in Pembrokeshire, Wales. It's the smallest city in the UK and is famed for its stunning coastline.

It was here where we had the most memorable encounter with a hobby, and it's an experience I will always treasure.

It was 31 August 2020, and Tracey and I were taking my mother's dog Gem on her usual 'before tea' walk. This trail was near the city, off the beaten track, taking you down into the valley where the cathedral sits. At this time of year we regularly see lots of butterflies, flowers, small birds, and all types of bees along this beautiful route.

This time things were different. I had lost my mother four days previously to cancer, which was very sudden and I was feeling very emotional and shocked.

But this isn't the only reason that I now remember this particular walk so vividly: something surprising happened that day, unlike anything I've experienced before.

We were crossing the field, coming up to the gate, when Tracey said, 'Anna, look!'
'What?'

Tracey pointed and suddenly I saw. There, just sitting on the gatepost and looking at us, was a hobby! She was quite small, puffed out, with beautiful markings that initially led me to believe she was a peregrine falcon. Her relaxed demeanour made it obvious she wasn't afraid in the slightest.

Apart from being wowed, my first thought was that something might be wrong with her, sitting there like she was. It was an unusual sight and odd behaviour for a hobby.

I carefully took a couple of pictures and said that if she was still there when we came back on our loop, then we would call someone I knew who would be able to help her. But I really hoped she was OK.

When we returned about 10–15 minutes later, she was indeed still there. Undisturbed, she watched us walk over and returned our gaze without any hint of fear. I tried to see if there was any indication that she was injured, but couldn't see anything concerning.

As I admired her, I noticed a few fluffy feathers among her plumage, and came to the conclusion that she was a young hobby and that she hadn't learnt to be wary of humans yet.

I'll never forget the way she looked at me ... I struggle to find the words to describe it and how it made me feel. We looked at one another and I felt a connection with this wild thing.

Young hobby. (© Anna Gilbert-Falconer)

After about ten minutes, she alighted from the gatepost and glided over to the next one, before taking one last look at me and flying away. To my relief, there was nothing wrong with her.

As I look back at this extraordinary event, I now believe that it was a sign from my mother. She loved wildlife, knew the names of the birds, and knew what time of day I'd be taking that walk. Through the hobby, she was making sure that I was still walking her little Gem, that we were all OK, and was letting me know that she was watching over me. It gives me so much comfort.

Where to see them

Hobbies can be seen in the UK in spring and summer, breeding in all regions of England, southern Scotland and eastern and southern Wales. It is an irregular summer visitor to Ireland and there is no evidence yet of it breeding there.

Hobby with catch. (© Graham Parkinson)

When searching for hobbies, look for them hunting over woodland and heathland, where there are plenty of insects. In late summer, gravel pits or other wetland environments are good places to try, as there will be an abundance of insect food there for hobbies.

The best time of day to see hobbies hunting is usually in the early morning or just before dusk. If you perceive a whirlwind of screaming birds, it may be a flock under attack from a hobby. Look out for its anchor-like shape in the sky and its shining white cheek and neck, both noticeable from a distance.

RSPB reserves to check out include Rainham Marshes in Essex, Ham Wall in Glastonbury, Fen Dayton Lakes in Cambridge, Langford Lowfields in Newark, Amberley Wildbrooks in the South Downs National Park and Surlingham Church Marsh in Norwich. An excellent place in Wales to see hobbies is at Newport Wetlands National Nature Reserve.

The channel Wildlife Windows on YouTube had a camera on a hobby nest in Dorset during the summer of 2022, making it possible to watch growing hobby chicks online. Search for it during the next breeding season to see if they have returned!

You can also try Amwell Nature Reserve in Hertfordshire and RSPB Arne in Dorset. The latter has nest cams on birds, including the hobby.

CHAPTER 5

Buzzard

Scientific name	*Buteo buteo*
Family	*Accipitridae* (kites, hawks and eagles)
UK conservation status	Green

History and current situation

As with most of our birds of prey, the buzzard has suffered prolonged persecution at the hands of man and has been impacted by pesticide pollution and reduced food resources.

In the 1700s, the UK boasted good numbers of buzzards, which were common and widely distributed. But in the middle of the century, game rearing became popular and during the 1800s, it was one of the principal activities in the British countryside. For this reason, gamekeepers and farmers began to shoot and trap buzzards, alongside other birds of prey, believing them to be a threat to the game (for example pheasants and rabbits) that they wished to save for their own hunting, food and monetary purposes.

After being exterminated in central and eastern parts of Britain, the buzzard was then classed as a protected species; however, this was largely ignored and did not protect its numbers. By the 1900s, buzzard numbers were at their lowest levels. At this time, a BTO atlas survey found that the highest number of buzzards could be found in Devon, Cornwall, and in central and western Wales. Good numbers could also be found in western Scotland and the Lake District. In Ireland, numbers were low: the buzzard had been completely exterminated there, but individuals had since drifted across from south-west Scotland and were beginning to recolonise the country.

During and following the two world wars, the buzzard experienced less persecution due to a fall in gamekeeper numbers and was able to begin recovering some of its lost ground. By the early 1950s it was even thought that buzzard numbers (8,000–12,000 territorial pairs) might be higher than they were in the early 1800s.

Buzzard. (© Russell Sherriff)

This was boosted by statutory legislation in 1954 that granted it, and other birds of prey, full protection. However, there was a setback when the fast-spreading *myxoma* virus infected rabbit populations, destroying a food source so important to the buzzard. Buzzard numbers saw dramatic declines over the succeeding years, with places including south-west England seeing a reduction of 50%. The total national population of buzzards in the late 1950s was estimated to be 6,000–8,000 pairs, and the bird became extinct in Ireland again.

A slow recovery took place from the 1960s, stunted in part by the impact of pesticides including DDT being used by farmers, especially in areas like the New Forest and the Lake District. The toxins in contaminated crops, and Dieldrin used in sheep-dips to prevent pest infestation, travelled up the food chain to these birds – leaving them with fragile, thin eggshells that resulted in lost or less successful clutches, thus supressing the number of new birds for several years. Fortunately, the buzzard's varied diet, which includes small mammals (who are able to metabolise and secrete organochlorines, and therefore do not accumulate these harmful chemicals within their bodies), meant that it suffered much less than specialist avian-eating birds of prey such as the sparrowhawk and peregrine falcon. In the 1970s, the use of DDTs was restricted and then eventually phased out.

The Wildlife and Countryside Act 1981 provided greater protection for all birds of prey. In 1983, of the estimated 12,000–17,000 buzzard pairs in the UK, almost half were found in Scotland, with a third in England and a quarter in Wales. From 1990, their numbers increased in many areas, and they began to spread further across

Buzzard soaring. (© Russell Sherriff)

southern and central parts of England, particularly due to landowners and farmers being more tolerant of their presence, and even interested in their conservation. They also coexisted, with little competition, alongside the red kites that had recently begun to recolonise these regions. (Indeed, the two are able to share woodlands for nesting and only fight sometimes over carrion.) The story was different in east Scotland and the Pennines, where buzzards were still being persecuted and poisoned, especially on large gaming estates.

In 2000, the BTO estimated that the UK had 31,000–44,000 territorial pairs, rising to 57,000–79,000 in 2009. It is worth pointing out that although buzzards have returned to their former homelands, the landscape of many of these places is significantly different to what existed in the 1700s. The swathes of intensely farmed countryside and urban sprawl, as well as the disappearance of woodlands in eastern and central England, means much less room and resources for all wildlife. This habitat is poor in invertebrate, small mammal and small bird food sources, but rich in larger prey such as rabbits and grey squirrels. Rabbits are still vulnerable to outbreaks of disease, so as they fluctuate buzzard numbers will too.

With its population having quadrupled since 1970, the buzzard is currently the most common diurnal bird of prey in Britain, superseding the now-declining kestrel.

Description, characteristics and behaviour

The buzzard could be considered the UK's drabbest bird of prey. However, on closer inspection, it is really rather handsome. I challenge anyone to look at its large, chestnut-coloured eyes and mottled, streaked and barred underside (that is lighter and more striking than its uniformly brown upper side) and disagree with me. The buzzard is best appreciated when perched, or when you can look up at it as it flies above you.

Although this general description covers most buzzards, there are, of course, variations in their colouring, including individuals who are partly or even fully white – in the case of leucistic individuals – and patterning can vary extensively between individuals across the UK.

Juveniles are even more patterned, with pale, spotted chests, throats and bellies, and have lighter irises. It takes around three years for juveniles to acquire their adult plumage.

Sturdily built, buzzards are an average 46–58cm in length and have a wingspan of 113–128cm. The male buzzard can weigh up to 1kg and the female up to 1.3kg. They both have powerful yellow legs with long, sharp talons, and a robust beak that is

Pale buzzard in flight. (© Russell Sherriff)

yellow near the nostrils, but greyish black in the main. Visually, the buzzard can be confused with the golden eagle, although the latter is much larger and generally only found in Scotland and Ireland.

The buzzard's call is usually the first thing that makes you aware of its presence in the sky. It emits a loud mewing *keee-ya* that can be heard for miles; buzzards sing out to each other as they search for food.

The buzzard soars grandly on broad, rounded, outstretched wings – holding them in a shallow 'V' shape – in wide, sweeping circles; its primary tips ('fingers') spread out and its barred tail feathers fanned out. The bird's whitish underparts can be admired from this viewpoint, along with the deep brown tips of its feathers – the latter forming a dark border along the edge of its wings. At times the buzzard may appear to hover in the air, kestrel-like, as it scans the ground for prey – but it is actually hanging suspended in an updraught of air, with its head facing into the wind. In this way the buzzard can float, needing little to no movement of its wings.

Sometimes a buzzard will perform acrobatics, either with another of its kind, or when bothered by a disgruntled crow that wants to move it on. It may dive steeply when making a kill, or when it is display diving (see next section).

The buzzard also likes to hunt from its favourite perches, such as on the limb of a dead tree.

Buzzard on pheasant carrion. (© Mark Hunter/Adobe Stock)

The buzzard enjoys a varied diet of small mammals (for example voles), small birds and any carrion it comes across. It eats reptiles and amphibians like adders and frogs too. In lean times, it resorts to eating earthworms and invertebrates. In certain areas (such as in the west), the buzzard predates larger birds such as corvids and pigeons. Rabbits are another important food source. Due to its opportunistic eating habits and flexible diet, the buzzard is able to survive in a variety of habitats.

The buzzard can be predated by foxes and wildcats, and is vulnerable to being sneaked up on by these while it is busy eating carrion. Where they exist in the same environment, eagles can catch and overpower them.

Buzzards reach an average age of 12 years in the wild, although the oldest known individual was 30 years old!

Habitat, nesting habits and breeding

The buzzard's ideal habitat, in which the species can reach the highest population densities, is on rich farmland amid a mix of deciduous woodland, hedgerows, grassland, scrub and pasture – environments that provide plentiful food. Population densities are lower in extensive conifer plantations, and in open moorland and mountain regions, where less food means that they have to spread over larger areas.

Buzzards usually mate for life and stay faithful to the territory they establish with their partner. A breeding pair bond through their aerial displays; the male and female sometimes touch talons mid-air. This tends to begin in February and March. To impress the female, the male flies upwards and then plummets in a dive back towards the earth in twists and turns, as part of his display.

In the countdown to egg laying, buzzards also engage in vocal courtship (for example, with a *pee-ya, pee-ya, pee-ya, pee-ya* call), select nest sites and nest build within woodlands. The tree that a pair chooses must be a reasonable size, with large forking branches in a sheltered and quiet location, with easy access and a good view of the surrounding area.

Buzzards create several nests to choose from and may even relocate early on if needed, although many stay loyal to a nest site for successive years. Other places where buzzards nest are on cliffs and mountains.

Around a week before egg laying, in early April, the male can be seen feeding the begging female, who calls *see-ee-yuk* from or near to the nest. She is conserving her energy and (usually) staying out of sight.

While she is incubating her clutch of two to three or up to six white eggs (that are sometimes marked with red splotches) for up to six weeks, she ceases flying almost completely. The male, meanwhile, guards the nest from nearby perches, patrolling the sky from above, and provides her with food. He needs to bring her the equivalent

Buzzard pair bonding in the sky. (© Chloé Valerie Harmsworth)

of ten short-tailed voles or one small rabbit each day. Before delivering the prey, he plucks them elsewhere, and sometimes partially eats the food – for example, he often eats the head of a small rabbit.

Once the chicks have hatched, the parents spend around eight weeks from mid-May to early July rearing their brood. The female spends most of her time on the nest until the chicks are around three weeks old, at which point she may leave it to hunt in the vicinity, when the weather is amenable. As the chicks increase in size and become more feathered, and are better at defending themselves from hassling crows, she can leave for longer periods to help gather much-needed food for her hungry, growing young.

By mid-July the young buzzards have fledged from their nest. Just before and just after this happens, their parents become increasingly vocal and aggressive when any threats come close to their young. At first, youngsters stay within the tree canopy and return to the nest for food, before gradually moving away from their natal home.

In late July to early August, fledglings make their first tentative flights above the tree line. These flights increase in frequency, length and confidence as they explore the territory, sometimes accompanied by their parents. They continue to be fed by the adults during August or even beyond this time, while they are learning to hunt invertebrates and small mammals from perches.

Buzzard on nest with chicks. (© WildMedia/Adobe Stock)

Eventually, usually in September, the juvenile buzzards spread out further away from the place they were born and become independent from their parents, ready to go it alone.

In the autumn, adult buzzards complete their annual moult and recover from the breeding season! It is now essential that they build up their fat reserves ready for winter.

Buzzards do not migrate from the UK – they stay with us year round as one of our resident birds of prey.

The brilliant buzzard

Written by Joe Harkness, naturalist and author of Bird Therapy *(Unbound, 2019).*

Every single time I see a buzzard circling above me, I am filled with the same feeling of chest-pounding adulation. The best way I can describe it is as an internal fist bump: this feeling of sheer joy each time I see one.

The buzzard doesn't even have to be in flight. Whether it is perched, grounded, jettisoning from a nearby tree or calling in the distance, I am grateful.

The buzzard's mewing call is a signal.

It's a reminder that anything is possible; that I can be better, that life can be better.

What is it about buzzards that conjure this state of mind in me? Well, maybe it is because they are a juxtaposition in themselves. Light and graceful as they glide across a blue summer sky; rigidly mechanical as they kettle together as a group on the thermals, seven-a-swirl, in June's heat haze. They are awkward, bulky, and feather-light.

The first time I really noticed buzzards was back when I was at the beginning of my still-ongoing recovery journey. It was a time when I was bound by my thought processes, mood swings and addiction. Up there in the sky, they were bound by nothing. I was gripped by their majesty.

Displaying over a treeline, dipping and rising, they represented freedom and a state of being that, at that time, seemed too far away for me to even comprehend.

I always use the word 'regal' when someone asks why they captivated me that day. It's hard to explain, but they seemed to be all that I aspired to be at that point. I'm careful not to attach human feelings to the winged kind, but they really, truly, gave me hope.

The increase in their numbers is startling. Ask older birders and they'll all say the same thing: 'I remember when you would hardly see them. Now they're everywhere.' It is much like the red kite, that other languid and grandiose bird of prey, which was previously so scarce that people would travel specifically to see them.

Buzzard coming in to land. (© ondrejprosicky/Adobe Stock)

Buzzard on a pole. (© George Cook)

This year, in 2022, we've had a buzzard over the garden or town most days throughout spring. Buzzards are more than just the red kite's noisy neighbours – they're ours now too.

And that's part of their enduring magic. I seem to see a buzzard at least once a day, usually on my drive to work. Most of the time it will be perched atop a telegraph pole; a sentinel of the arable fields that line my commute.

The rodent-watcher will sometimes burst from a tree along the road: swooping, soaring and with its legs dangling before tucking them in, as its uncomfortable flight becomes more fluid.

My reminder. Once a day. Every day.

Where to see them

Buzzards breed in every county of the UK and can be found year round in most types of habitat from woodland, pasture, marsh, towns (with sufficient green space) and villages, moorland, scrub and arable areas. In urban areas they can sometimes be seen perched on pylons or fence posts, which may be that particular individual's favourite spot to hunt from.

Buzzards can be seen visiting the same feeding stations as red kites, for example in mid-Wales. They can also be seen in wilder regions, such as the moors and mountains of the Western Scottish Islands and Highlands, North Wales and the Lake District, as well as the flatter and more intensely farmed central and eastern England. In winter, some individuals fly over to join the buzzard population in Ireland.

It is very unlikely that you will need to travel to see a buzzard – you probably have several living near you!

CHAPTER 6

Red Kite

Scientific name	*Milvus milvus*
Family	*Accipitridae* (kites, hawks and eagles)
UK Conservation Status	Green

'While, near the midway cliff, the silvered kite
In many a whistling circle wheels her flight'
An Evening Walk by William Wordsworth

History and current situation

In medieval London, the red kite was a common bird. It was protected by royal statute due to its usefulness in taking leftover scraps from the streets to eat, as well as rubbish to decorate its nest with (see page 82). However, the bird was a slight nuisance when it stole hung-out washing for its nest. This is referred to in Shakespeare's *The Winter's Tale*: 'when the kite builds, look to lesser linen'. It also wasn't unheard of for a red kite to snatch food from a person's hands, or a hat from their head. Back then, red kites and humans truly lived alongside each other and interacted that closely.

In the sixteenth century, attitudes towards the red kite changed. No longer well thought of, it became classed as vermin, with a bounty put on its head. This was the result of obsessive ideas about protecting game from any potential predator – a closed-minded and uneducated perspective that caused the decline of most our birds of prey. The red kite was mercilessly persecuted by being poisoned (often by contaminating the carrion it ate) or shot.

The cleaning up, draining and development of cities in the eighteenth century meant there were fewer opportunities for the red kite to hunt and breed. Red kites breeding in our towns and cities (such as in London's Grays Inn until 1777) became a thing of the past. The bird was no longer welcome in our cities or the countryside.

Stunning red kite. (© Chloé Valerie Harmsworth)

To compound the problem, there was an increase in its eggs being stolen by collectors as it became a rarer bird. The combination of these factors caused the red kite population to decline rapidly. By the late nineteenth century this beautiful bird – which had featured in several William Wordsworth poems in the previous century – was extinct in England and Scotland.

It was only in the hills and woods of the Upper Tywi valley in Wales that some red kites survived. By the late 1930s and early 1940s there were ten breeding pairs left in this area. But they were not safe here either: egg collectors, a limited genetic gene pool and a rain-drenched climate were among the serious challenges that this small population faced. This, certainly, was the lowest point in the red kite's history.

In 1981 legal protection for our native and threatened wildlife species (including wild birds, their nests and eggs) was put in place with the Wildlife and Countryside Act. Although persecution hasn't ceased completely, people caught causing harm are arrested and prosecuted. This deterrent has reduced the number of red kite deaths. Conservationists also decided to act before the red kite disappeared completely.

There were opposing views on what would be the most effective way to save the species. Some believed that the red kite should be directly reintroduced to a number of locations across the UK; others thought that efforts should be focused on protecting the remaining individuals in Wales, in the hope that they would spread further afield naturally. In the end, the reintroduction programme went ahead, with one reason being that red kites are sociable creatures, often reluctant to set up home in new areas, so it might not have been wise to rely on a natural spread from Wales.

Almost 1,000 young birds from Sweden, Spain and Germany (plus a few from Wales) were released at nine different sites in England and Scotland between 1989 and 2013. Once new populations became established, chicks were taken from these to be released at other sites. According to Ian Carter, author of *The Red Kite's Year* (and involved in the programme), the re-established population in the Chiltern Hills alone supplied '237 young for subsequent release projects'.

There was initial concern as to whether relocated birds would struggle in a landscape that had changed dramatically since the sixteenth century. Land clearances and urban development provided far fewer trees and woodland cover for nesting. Farming had transformed too, using intensive practices that could potentially be dangerous for the red kite and may have reduced its food sources.

And yet, from just 52 known nests in Wales in 1989, the red kite is now found in most English counties, with more than 5,000 breeding pairs in the UK. This growth far exceeded conservationists' expectations and shows just how adaptable this bird is. The programme is widely regarded as one of the finest examples of reintroduction in the UK.

The red kite's global population might benefit as well, as the descendants of our reintroduced birds could be used to replenish diminished populations in Europe. Success stories like this have inspired the reintroduction of other animal species across the UK and the world.

Red kite in flight. (© Russell Sherriff)

The year 2020 marked 30 years since the red kite's triumphant return to our skies. The project proves that we can make amends for past wildlife crimes and work towards restoring the UK's natural ecosystem. And the red kite population could flourish to an even greater extent: according to Ian Carter, our multiple areas of suitable countryside could support 'in excess of 50,000 pairs'. The bird is still persecuted, however, by misinformed people who regard it as a threat to game and livestock (see page 80 for information on the red kite's diet).

Due to its strong links to the country, many people consider the red kite to be the national bird of Wales.

Description, characteristics and behaviour

The red kite glides elegantly on the thermals, floating majestically through the air above our urban towns and over agricultural fields, while staring calmly at the world below. With its impressive size and look, humans who have not seen one before can mistake it for an eagle.

If you hear a piercing, high-pitched whistle from the sky and look up to see a large golden-brown bird with expansive wings, a forked tail and an eagle-like hooked beak, you are most likely looking at a red kite! This previously rare bird can now be seen almost everywhere in the UK and it is inextricably linked to humans, foraging around us and living in the woodlands on the edges of our towns.

Up close you would see that the red kite has a tawny or rusty, reddish brown body and a pale grey to whitish head patterned with dark vertical streaks. It has a yellow beak with a dark tip, and strikingly light, intelligent eyes, with a piercing, black pupil.

Its long, angular wings span 185cm on average. The upper sides of these are red-brown at the shoulders, followed by a paler band, with the rest of the feathers quite dark. The undersides are reddish at the shoulders, with a darker, blackish patch at its wrist, a brown section close to the body and a bold white section further from the body, with dark 'fingers' at their ends. Overall, the colouring and look of the red kite isn't too dissimilar to the male marsh harrier.

The red kite generally flies fairly high and slowly, with minimal effort and only infrequent, casual flaps of its wings. This characteristic, gliding flight gave the bird its name of *Gled* or *Glead* in northern England and Scotland, as noted by the pioneering naturalist Gilbert White in 1779.

The red kite's most distinctive feature is its long, forked tail. It uses this like a rudder to steer its direction in flight. The underside of the tail is pale in colour and its outer points are black-tipped. The tail helps to hold the red kite inside thermals while it scrutinises the ground below. The tail's span can be altered to widen or tighten the

Red kite turning into a dive. (© Russell Sherriff)

bird's turns in the sky – for example, a wide fork allows a sharp turn. This tail has led to the red kite's name of Fork Tail in Yorkshire and Crotch Tail in Essex.

Larger than the buzzard, the red kite is an average 61–72cm in length and has a wingspan of 175–195cm. It can weigh up to 1.3kg. The male and female look very similar. The male is slightly smaller and lighter, while the female has slightly longer, broader and more pointed wings, as well as a less deeply forked tail. This can only really be discerned (and it still isn't easy) if you see the two together. Juveniles have paler breasts and upper sides to their wings.

Despite its size, the red kite can perform aerial acrobatics – twisting and turning suddenly to re-examine something, or to drop to the ground with a sudden flex of speed.

The red kite hunts over fields, farmland, moorland and urban settings, and is a scavenger that mainly eats worms and carrion, although it is opportunistic and occasionally takes small mammals (for example voles and immature rabbits) and young birds when it can. It is able to dispatch small, live prey with its beak.

On farmland, the red kite follows ploughing and harvesting machinery, looking out for unearthed worms and small mammals; in urban and suburban environments, it can take scraps from gardens and roadkill. It pesters birds like corvids and other birds of prey, snatching the food that they drop. And, like the hobby, it hawks for crane flies and dragonflies. The red kite may therefore be the most adaptable bird of prey in the UK, with the most generalist diet.

It scavenges and purloins the catches of others because it is not as powerful as it looks. This is reflected in the hierarchy of carrion eating – there is a literal pecking order! Not possessing a beak strong enough to puncture the skin of a dead sheep or similar, the red kite must wait for other carrion eaters such as buzzards or ravens to do this. It waits its turn in the dinner queue.

As with many other birds of prey, the red kite's numbers can be linked to how well vole populations are doing. It also had a difficult time when *myxomatosis* in rabbits was at its peak.

Adult red kites are fortunately free from predators. The average lifespan of a wild red kite is ten years, although the oldest recorded was 26 years old!

The red kite's call is a *weieie-ee-oww* or *weeoo-weeoo-weeoo* that is higher-pitched than the buzzard's, but can sound similar. Its musical quality has given the bird the name *Boda Chwiw* – Whistling Kite – in Wales.

Habitat, nesting habits and breeding

The red kite lives in mixed-habitat environments of farmland, uplands, moorlands or towns with adjacent woodlands – areas with places to both nest and hunt.

Red kite aerial courtship. (© giedriius/Adobe Stock)

While the red kite hunts over open areas, it nests in woodlands. However, these must be roomy ones, since densely packed woodlands are no good for its forked tail, which would suddenly become a hindrance and susceptible to damage. (The goshawk has a straight tail and is therefore better adapted to dense woodlands.) The red kite requires space between the trees for it to fly safely in and out of the woodland, as well as ample room around its nest.

Only the area immediately around the nest is the red kite's territory; it is far less territorial than many other birds of prey. The bird's tolerant and gregarious nature means that a locality can end up with high densities of red kites. This is why you can sometimes look up and see many of them flying simultaneously. Outside of the breeding season, red kites will even forage in loose groups, and roost as pairs or in small communities during the winter.

In early spring, the male and female fly in courtship – one above the other – mirroring each other's movements. Or they will fly one behind the other with deep, exaggerated wing beats, followed by a vigorous chase. They may also dramatically lock claws and cartwheel through the air in a heart-stopping performance!

Red kites begin to breed at two years old. Once paired, they are usually monogamous and return to the same nest each breeding season. This nest is often built on top of an old crow or buzzard nest, high in a tree (around 12–20m above the ground). It is a very untidy bundle of medium to large sticks, lined with sheep's wool, grass, or other soft materials. The pair contribute to the nest throughout the breeding season and add new material to it when they reuse it the following year (if the nest was successful). Over time, the nest grows to a considerable size.

The pair affix colourful and shiny objects to the edge of the nest, possibly to help with locating the nest, or to mark it as their own. They have been known to take all sorts of items for this purpose from washing to other fabrics, plastic bags, crisp packets and scraps of plastic.

In April, the female lays a clutch of around three eggs, at three-day intervals. The eggs are non-glossy and creamy white, with red-brown spots. The female stays with the eggs while the male provides the food. She incubates them for just over a month each, until they begin to hatch over several days.

Egg laying (and hatching) is perfectly timed so that young red kites can be fed on the glut of young corvids, wood pigeons and gulls around at this time. Likewise, red kite chicks can be predated by adult corvids and other birds of prey.

For the first two weeks, the male is the primary food provider. After this, the female shares the hunting duties and the parents place food on the nest for the young to feed themselves.

When they are 45 days old, the red kite chicks begin to wander from the nest into other parts of the tree, still being fed by their parents. They don't fully fledge from this

Red kite on its nest. (© Chloé Valerie Harmsworth)

tree until they are around 48 to 50 days old, or older. Even then, the parents continue to feed them for up to 20 additional days.

When independent juveniles leave, they may fly many miles away; however, they often return to their natal area when they are ready to breed.

Red kites are UK residents year round and do not migrate.

My local red kites
Written by Chloé Valerie Harmsworth.

Red kites bring a thrilling wildness to the suburban habitat in which I live. Soaring above my red brick mid-terrace house, they remind me of what awaits beyond the horizon: open fields; expansive skies; sprawling woodlands. By moving beyond my perceived boundaries, I can be as free as the birds that stir my soul.

The red kite first appeared to me in 2017 when I was about to move from a house I'd been unhappy in to one a stone's throw away from my childhood home. Just days before this change, I saw from my bedroom window (with packing boxes all around me) two red kites flying in a joyful, exuberant dance. They were twisting and turning in tandem and I couldn't tear my eyes away. I realise now that this was a pair performing a courtship display (see page 81).

That scene felt like a promise of better times ahead – of life moving in the right direction. I'd never seen a red kite before and suddenly it was a very important bird to me. I was immediately enamoured.

Luckily that first glimpse wasn't the last. Miles away at my new house, I soon frequently saw a red kite flying overhead, calling. He, who I call Roger, must be one of the descendants of the 13 Spanish red kites released in the Chiltern Hills in July 1990. Although my childhood had been full of exciting nature encounters, I had no memories of seeing red kites, and this was because they hadn't reached my Hertfordshire town yet.

I regularly see two, sometimes three, red kites circling over the fields close to my home, and slightly further afield, I've witnessed six of them flying low over a farm. My ears are so attuned to the bird's whistling call that my head snaps to the sky whenever I hear it. There aren't many things more glorious than a gliding red kite glowing in the sunshine.

During the Covid lockdowns, the red kite began to represent future freedom as well as hope. As the world underwent this immensely challenging period, I had to believe that with care and strength we could endure and recover, just like the red kite had.

In early 2021, while walking through a nearby spinney, I discovered that my local red kite pair had a nest there. I made return visits to check on their progress, with weeks between so as not to disturb them. Several times I was able to watch (at a distance, through my binoculars, while hidden behind an elder tree and camouflaged in my '90s parka jacket) one of the pair sitting on the nest.

This was at the pre-egg laying stage; the nest was a large jumble of sticks encrusted with bright green and yellow lichen. It looked incredibly unconsidered in its arrangement, as if it had been dumped there without much care. Could it really be structurally sound enough to hold delicate eggs or young safely, let alone an adult or two on top of it? It seemed unlikely. Adding to its ramshackle appearance were the infamous red kite accoutrements: in this case, bits of plastic sheeting and locks of wool. On sunny days the former reflected the light and on overcast days the latter glowed like a beacon in the gloom.

I didn't know whether this pair had used the nest successfully in the past, or if this was a first attempt for a young, new pair. Either way, when breeding season arrived, I became an increasingly cautious observer. If they spotted me and left the nest, or flew over the spinney calling incessantly, I would leave. It was their home after all and I didn't want them to abandon it.

I visited them even less as we moved further into spring and, by the time summer came, there was little point anyway as the abundant foliage had obscured the nest totally. I hoped that they had laid eggs and were successfully rearing their chicks; that the dodgy-looking nest was sheltering new red kites.

When the leaves fell away again and the nest was revealed once more, I didn't see red kites in the spinney much. There was a very real sense of emptiness there – like the life and soul of the party had gone. I knew that they were now probably spending most of their time foraging or hiding out of sight.

Red kite nest with wool on its edges. (© Chloé Valerie Harmsworth)

However, one day I did come across a red kite there, grooming himself. He was sitting on a branch at the edge of the spinney, right by the path. I was at the base of the tree, frozen stock-still in surprise; I had only spotted him last-minute. He hadn't noticed me and continued to preen.

It was a privilege to watch this personal act of self-care. His neck twisted around as he pulled his back, tail and wing feathers through his beak to remove any unwanted parasites like lice or tics, and to straighten and smooth any ragged plumes.

He pulled amusing faces as he did this – bring to your mind the goofy expression of a cat or dog having a great scratch! That was until, through his half-closed eyes, his pupils focused on the sight of me, far below. His eyes widened in shock, and I could have sworn that there was a fleeting, embarrassed expression as he realised that I had been spying on his private moment. He flew off with a perturbed flick of his forked tail.

Another time I saw him at a distance deep within the spinney, half hidden in the shadows of a wet winter's day. He sat straight and still as a statue, his feathers soggy and bedraggled. I couldn't help but think he looked fed up at not being able to look presentable in those conditions!

From that first sighting in 2017, the red kite has been a symbol of luck and hope to me, especially during difficult times. One always appears when I need cheering

Red kite spotting me mid-preen. (© Chloé Valerie Harmsworth)

up, and it reminds me not to give up. It's an exhilarating burst of nature that encourages me to go outside and reconnect with the wild world that continues to shape me.

I wrote the following poem to express my admiration for the red kite and to imagine what it would be like to be reincarnated as one.

When I finally leave this place
By Chloé Valerie Harmsworth

When I finally leave this place
That has held me for so long
Will I be a bird of grace
Or be a bird of song?

Will I be suspended
In the air so out of reach
And when my time is ended
Will your call succeed my speech?

Shall my feet transform to claw
My blue eyes pale to white
Will I embody what I adore
With wind my new delight?

Shall my nose and mouth remould as beak
My skin and hair convert to feather
My eyes sharpen for food I seek
Connected to sky forever?

A symbol of strength I would become
Restored from distant history
A rare sight now known by everyone
If 'you' became 'me'.

Your shape has brought me endless joy
As well as awe and wonder
So when my body begins to cloy
And it's time to leave it under,

Perhaps my soul will rearrange
My form as I've described
And I won't find it hard or strange
To leave the soil to which I'm tied,

And finally I will leave this place
Shedding my worthless fear
And love and hope with it replace
With you, my friend, quite near.

Where to see them

Red kites can be found in the UK throughout the year.

They are one of the easiest birds of prey to see as they are widespread across the UK and live happily alongside us in both urban and rural environments.

The most likely place to see them is in the air. The forked tails of their silhouettes in the sky make them fairly easy to recognise and distinguish from other birds of prey. Once spotted, you will usually have the luxury of following them with your eyes for a while, with ample time to take in their beauty (and potentially exciting acrobatics). They are not a dash-and-hide bird like some others. They are rarely bothered by us

Red kite sitting in a tree. (© Graham Parkinson)

outside of the nesting/breeding season, and when flying above may even appear to be looking at you with intelligent interest (I certainly perceive this).

You might become aware of a red kite above you after hearing its call, or the noise of corvids pushing it out of the area. Or you might see one flying through or over woodland. When it is resting or the conditions for flying aren't right, you might come across one sitting in a tree.

The best regions to see red kites are central England – especially the Chilterns – central Wales and central Scotland (at Argaty and along the Galloway Kite Trail). In Northern Ireland, red kites are spreading out slowly from their core range in County Down.

As scavengers, red kites can be drawn in large numbers to places where humans leave rubbish, or put out food. For example, hundreds gather at the Red Kite Feeding Centre at Gigrin Farm in Wales, which you can visit.

Red kite on carrion. (© Paolo/Adobe Stock)

THE SECRET LIFE OF BIRDS OF PREY

CHAPTER 7

Harriers

HEN HARRIER

Scientific name	*Circus cyaneus*
Family	*Accipitridae* (kites, hawks and eagles)
UK conservation status	Red

History and current situation

The hen harrier bears the unfortunate title of the most persecuted bird of prey in the UK. This is due to its predation of free-ranging fowl: the 'harrying' of them leading to its common name. This natural inclination has resulted in the hen harrier being targeted regularly, especially on grouse moors, where they are killed illegally by landowners and gamekeepers to protect the grouse they keep there for field sports. In the nineteenth century, hen harrier numbers were decimated, and unfortunately this discrimination continues today despite the species being protected by law.

Among other prey items, the hen harrier does predate game birds – generally the younger and weaker of the stock – but it is perfectly possible to manage these environments in order for both to live side by side. A healthy ecosystem involves all the creatures in the food chain, each playing its vital role. This stunning bird deserves to exist here and should be allowed and encouraged to re-establish its natural territories, free from traps, poisoning, shooting and egg collectors.

The destruction of suitable habitat has also played a significant part in the hen harrier's decline, with much of their landscape being taken over by commercial forestry.

Natural causes that affect the hen harrier are the predation of its eggs and young in their ground-level nest by animals such as foxes and bitterns, and heavy spring rainfalls that flood or destroy the nest. The hen harrier is reliant on vole populations

Male hen harrier flying. (© Russell Sherriff)

too – a crash in the number of voles can mean that the hen harrier cannot get enough to eat.

In 2012, there were 617 hen harrier pairs in the UK – 20% fewer than in 2004. And in 2013, no chicks successfully fledged in England. It has therefore been necessary for conservationists to monitor hen harrier numbers, provide additional food sources, protect their nests and winter roosts, and work towards reintroducing them to suitable areas of south England (potentially using chicks from high-density areas).

As a result, hen harrier fledging numbers have increased gradually since 2013. In 2022, 49 nests were recorded across Cumbria, Yorkshire, Lancashire, Northumberland and Country Durham, with 34 of these successfully producing chicks. For the first time in over a century, hen harrier fledging numbers in the uplands of England exceeded 100 in one breeding season (119 in total).

Although this is very encouraging and testament to the dedicated conservation work carried out on the hen harrier's behalf, there is still a long way to go before numbers are where they would naturally be without illegal persecution.

Educational and fundraising events such as the annual Hen Harrier Day and Hen Harrier Fest aim to help raise awareness and appreciation for this bird. Dr Ruth

Tingay, founder of the Raptor Persecution UK blog and co-director of Wild Justice (alongside Chris Packham CBE and Dr Mark Avery), often speaks at these events. On 31 August 2022, she stated on her blog that 'at least 72 hen harriers have been killed since 2018', so there is clearly much more to be done to end this horrific victimisation.

Description, characteristics and behaviour

The female hen harrier is brown and creamy white, with a white rump and a long, barred tail, earning her the name of Ringtail. The juveniles share this feature, although their barring is less distinct.

   The male meanwhile is pale grey, slimmer than the female, with black wing tips and a subtler white rump. His tail does not feature distinct bars. His light, almost bluish colour is referred to by the word *cyaneus* in the bird's scientific name. Because of this, he is known as the Blue Hawk or Blue Kite in Scotland and Wales. In Hampshire he is known as the Grey Buzzard. Due to his faint resemblance to a gull, he is called the Seagull Hawk in Ireland. Hauntingly, he is described as the Grey Ghost in many places.

   Both sexes have bright yellow eyes and flat faces that make them look almost owl-like when viewed straight on. Due to the difference in feather coloration, the male and female were once believed to be two separate species.

   Hen harriers are 44–52cm in length, with a wingspan of 100–120cm. The male weighs 300–400g while the female is larger at 400–600g.

Female hen harrier flying. (© Russell Sherriff)

The hen harrier tends to fly low and slow, gliding with the wind and holding its wings in a shallow 'V' shape, with just the odd flap, as it searches for food below. It flies closer to the ground than the marsh harrier, hugging the contours of the landscape, and sometimes even trails its long legs through tall grass or heather. It circles the same hunting area repeatedly, as indicated by *circus* – which comes from the Greek *kirkos*, meaning 'ring' or 'circle' – in its scientific name. However, its hunting area is usually larger than the marsh harrier's.

The hen harrier has an exceptional sense of hearing. Its flat, disc-like face and pronounced facial ruff are extremely efficient sound detectors, picking up the tiny noises of small mammals moving invisibly along their grassy tunnels. With potential prey aurally pinpointed, the hen harrier speeds up its flight to gain the element of surprise, before stalling suddenly to achieve the correct angle and swooping down to seize the creature with its deadly talons.

The most common hen harrier prey is small birds and mammals, such as meadow pipits, voles, rats, and rabbits (the latter taken by the larger female). It takes young moorland waders as well. The hen harrier has also been observed hunting bats where these are available. As mentioned previously, voles are an important food source to the hen harrier and changes in the numbers of these can cause fluctuations in hen harrier populations.

The hen harrier's calls include a wailing or squealing whistle or a series of soft *ke-ke-ke-ke* notes.

It rarely lives beyond eight years, though one was recorded in the wild at 16 years old. Its natural predators include foxes and golden eagles.

Habitat, nesting habits and breeding

The hen harrier favours hillsides of bracken, heather moorlands and heathlands. In Sussex, it is known as the Gorse Harrier, after the spiky plant with coconut-scented flowers that grows in these environments.

During the breeding season, which runs from April to July, both the male and female will perform their famous sky dance. The attributes of this are a series of rises and falls: the bird climbing high into the air and corkscrewing back towards the earth in dizzying spirals, over and over. The hen harrier's steep undulations are believed to be deeper than those of the marsh harrier. The male and female emit a bouncy *chuk-uk-uk-uk* as they wheel through the air, and exchange tokens of affection in the sky to cement their bond. This display also reminds others of their territory.

Hen harriers usually form monogamous pairs, though there are exceptions to this rule. For example, on the island of Orkney in Scotland, there exists a population of hen harriers that are renowned for being polygynous. The males mate with multiple females, anywhere from three to seven of them! In this situation, the females have to hunt more frequently, as the males are spread thinly over several broods.

Hen harriers nest on a mound of vegetation or dirt on the ground, concealed within a thicket. The nest is made from sticks and lined with leaves and grass. Where an Orcadian male has a harem of females, these nests may be as little as 50m apart. The hen harrier's excellent hearing comes in useful when listening out for threats from this vulnerable nest. The alarm call it uses in response to intruders is a *chit-it-it-it-it-et-it*.

The female lays between four to eight whitish eggs over one- to three-day intervals in April or May and incubates them for a month. During this time, the male provides her with food, which she receives with a whistling *piih-eh* call.

Once the chicks have hatched, the male rarely watches over them, but he helps to feed them by passing food to the female – often transferring it to her mid-air so that the exact nest location isn't made obvious – for her to feed to the young. When the chicks are a little older, the female returns to hunting and drops food onto the nest from above, for the chicks to consume.

Their feathers start growing at around 15 days old, at which point the young move off the nest into nearby vegetation. From these hiding places they call to their parents for food. Thirty-six days after hatching, the young are ready to fully fledge, although they may remain reliant on the female for an extra couple of weeks.

Female juveniles won't reproduce until they are around two years old; the males take three years to reach sexual maturity.

Hen harrier chicks. (© Vladimir Konjushenko/Adobe Stock)

In winter hen harriers tend to move southwards, where they roost communally, sometimes with marsh harriers and merlins, and spend most of their time hunting. They return to their breeding grounds in March or April.

On the island of Orkney, the hen harriers can stay where they are, as there is a bountiful supply of the Orkney vole.

Read about the exciting moment a hen harrier clashed with a merlin on page 51.

Where to see them

During the breeding season, look out for hen harriers hunting over moorlands and similarly remote, rural habitats. You may be lucky enough to witness their exhilarating sky dance. In Northern Ireland, try the Antrim hills and Fermanagh uplands.

Hen harrier strongholds include north and west Scotland, the Isle of Man and Shetland. Also Orkney, which runs excellent guided tours.

The hen harrier has increased its range down from Scotland and into the northern counties of England: Cumbria, Yorkshire, Lancashire, Northumberland and Country Durham. One of the largest populations of hen harrier can be found in the Forest of Bowland in rural Lancashire.

In winter, hen harriers often desert their upland breeding grounds and move southwards. They can be seen in Wales during this time in places such as Cors Ddyga in Anglesey.

Hunting male hen harrier. (© dennisjacobsen/Adobe Stock)

MARSH HARRIER

Scientific name	*Circus aeruginosus*
Family	*Accipitridae* (kites, hawks and eagles)
UK conservation status	Amber

History and current situation

As with most of our other birds of prey, the marsh harrier has experienced prolonged persecution at the hands of man. Although there was a brief respite during the two world wars, it came under threat again when wildfowlers returned to the marshes. The population was also hit hard by persistent egg collecting.

Further to this, changes in land use impacted the marsh harrier greatly: the draining of wetlands and fenlands, especially during the eighteenth and nineteenth

Male marsh harrier. (© Bob Cooper)

centuries, reduced the amount of suitable habitat available to the bird. In Ireland, for example, around 80% of fens were lost to drainage for peat extraction or converted into agricultural land, and the bird became extinct in the country by 1918.

The intentional flooding of coastal land in the UK (to prevent invasion) during the Second World War helped the bird somewhat; and more areas became habitable for it following tidal surges in Norfolk and Suffolk in 1953.

By 1958, England had 15 marsh harrier nests. Then pesticides then came in, with their devastating consequences. By 1971, there was only one marsh harrier nest left in England, restricted to one small corner of the Norfolk Broads. The marsh harriers here struggled to move into neighbouring areas to increase their range and numbers, on account of the persecution they met there.

For decades, the marsh harrier had the undesirable distinction of being the UK's rarest bird of prey – rarer even than the red kite, which seems unbelievable.

When persecution relented as further laws came in, marsh harriers were finally able to spread naturally and increase their numbers. The banning of certain pesticides helped too. Over the last 20 years, the breeding population of marsh harriers has made a recovery, particularly along the east and south-east coast of England. More secure now than at any other time during the last century, there are currently around 600–700 breeding pairs in the UK.

Continued protection of the marsh harrier and other birds of prey is needed, particularly in places such as North Yorkshire, the UK's hotspot for confirmed cases of bird of prey persecution. Landscape restoration is also essential, especially in Ireland, due to the scale of habitat loss.

Description, characteristics and behaviour

At 48–56cm in length, with a wingspan of 115–130cm, the marsh harrier has a heavier build and broader wings than the hen harrier. It also lacks the hen harrier's white rump.

The male marsh harrier weighs 400–660g and the female 540–800g.

The male's wings are similar to the red kite's: brown in the armpits, moving into a lighter cream, white or blue-grey colour, before ending with black tips. His body is brown but his head and neck are lighter, streaked with brown. He has a yellow eye, with a dark pupil. His legs are yellow, his tail light grey, and his hooked beak is yellow tipped with black.

The female is a lot darker, with blackish brown feathers all over, except for her obviously creamy or silver head and neck. She bears a dark stripe through her eyes and a dark patch on her cheeks. She has brown eyes and yellow legs.

Juveniles are chocolate brown with a light crown and throat; young males have the plumage characteristics of both sexes.

Interestingly, some male marsh harriers end up with female plumage colouring; it is their yellow eyes and smaller size that confirms their sex in this case.

The Latin *aeruginosus* in the marsh harrier's scientific name means 'rusty', referring to the bird's colouring. As with the hen harrier, *circus* refers to the bird's habit of circling the same hunting area over and over.

Other names given to the marsh harrier include Duck Hawk in Ireland due to their predilection for waterfowl, *Bog Gled* (Glider of the Bog) in East Lothian and Bald Buzzard in Essex. The latter is likely due to the female's pale head looking almost bald (from a distance) compared to the brown feathers of her body.

Wiltshire folklore says rain is on its way when a large number of marsh harriers alight on the downs.

The marsh harrier's flight is light and it holds its wings in a shallow 'V'. It has a long, straight, non-forked tail. It hunts low over wetlands (generally 2–6m above the ground, slightly higher than the hen harrier), scrutinising field margins, long grass and reed beds. It can calmly lift itself over fences, hedges and other obstacles, using the wind to hold it up – turning into it whenever it needs to slow or stabilise its flight. The marsh harrier meticulously checks a patch repeatedly, not extending its search over as wide an area as the hen harrier.

Female marsh harrier hunting at Rainham Marshes. (© Pete Woods; see story on page 100)

Its serene flight makes it mesmerising to watch, and the close proximity of its body to the ground can make the bird appear larger than it is.

When soaring and gliding high in the air, its shape is similar to the buzzard, although it has a straighter line to its outstretched wings.

Despite being a large bird, the marsh harrier usually only takes small prey. It is, however, a generalist feeder: small mammals, birds, amphibians and even crustaceans, fish and insects all provide useful sustenance. The marsh harrier only specialises if there is a particular abundance or glut of a prey item – for example, the marsh frogs at Rainham Marshes (see page 103).

In the summer months, young rabbits, moorhens and coots are also on the menu. The marsh harrier conducts unrelenting dive-bomb attacks to exhaust and drown the birds – much harsher behaviour than its Kent nickname of Coot-Teaser lets on!

It occasionally consumes carrion, as its size means that it can compete with other carrion eaters such as buzzards, red kites and corvids. At times the marsh harrier takes larger birds (for example ducks or snipe) when a good opportunity arises, but these don't tend to form a big part of its diet.

Unlike most other birds of prey, the marsh harrier doesn't just use its eyesight to locate prey – it uses its excellent sense of hearing as well. During its low hunting

Male marsh harrier hunting at Rainham Marshes. (© Pete Woods; see story on page 100)

flight, it can pick up rustles and squeaks in the undergrowth. The ruff on its face – which it can puff out to increase efficiency – channels sound into the large ear openings behind its eyes. After the prey has been detected aurally, the marsh harrier uses its eyes to home in on its target. Only the hen harrier is more advanced at this (see page 92).

The female marsh harrier focuses her hunt over the reed bed, while the paler male also hunts over open ground – since he blends in better with the sky, he is less noticeable to prey.

Often the marsh harrier spots its prey having already flown over it, and performs a split-second somersault before dropping down to catch it. As it descends, the bird holds its wings back and reaches out with its long legs and large feet. It grabs its victim by wrapping its front and back talons around it, puncturing the creature on both sides of its body. Using its strong beak, the marsh harrier skins mammals and plucks birds, before removing their skin.

The marsh harrier's success rate when hunting is thought to be 15–27%, which is higher than the average 5–10% of most birds of prey.

The marsh harrier's call is a sharp and short *kwii-uuu* note that goes up and then down in pitch.

The marsh harrier lives for an average of six years, although the oldest recorded in the wild was 16 years old!

Habitat, nesting habits and breeding

The marsh harrier's natural habitats are wetlands, fenlands, marine and intertidal environments. It is the bird of prey that most relies on a specific type of habitat. Reed beds are essential to it for hunting and nesting. It is so connected to these that in France it is known as *Le Busard des Roseaux* – the Harrier of the Reeds.

Marsh harriers carry out their courtship acrobatics just above the reed beds. The male gives a nuptial gift to his partner: a small mammal, passed to her mid-air.

The breeding season begins from mid-March, when the male pairs with up to three females. While some pairs remain loyal to one another for several years in a row, others only pair up for a single breeding season.

Marsh harriers nest on the ground, concealed within the reed beds. The nest is composed of reeds, sticks and grasses. While the female sets up the real nest, the male constructs two false ones nearby.

The marsh harrier's excellent hearing comes in useful when listening out for threats from this vulnerable, non-elevated position. It is aided by its environment too: the crackle of reeds alerts it to incoming predators, such as foxes or bitterns. Reeds are not

Above left: *Female marsh harrier about to land in reeds. (© Zakaria Laperashvili/Adobe Stock)*
Above right: *Marsh harrier chicks from incoming female's perspective. (© Vaclav/Adobe Stock)*

easy vegetation to move through, especially for humans. This helps to give the marsh harrier the privacy it requires, which is very important as it can be quick to abandon the nest if disturbed.

In late April, the female lays three to eight eggs at two- to three-day intervals. The eggs are oval-shaped and white, with a blue or green tinge when first laid. She incubates these for at least a month until they hatch; the male provides the food. The male continues doing this after the eggs hatch; the female feeds the chicks with the food he has supplied.

The young marsh harriers fledge 31–38 days later, although the female tends to them for a further 15–25 days.

During their learning period, juveniles will chase almost anything. Eventually, however, they learn which techniques work best and which prey is worthwhile.

Marsh harriers are classically migratory, leaving our shores in September or October, and yet an increasing number (usually the females) are staying in the UK year round, along the coastal areas, due to our now milder winters. Those that still migrate return to their UK breeding sites by April.

The Rainham marsh harriers
Written by Howard Vaughan, former Visitor Experience Officer at RSPB Rainham Marshes in Essex.

Back in July 2000, the RSPB purchased just over 1,000 acres of land along the Thames from the Ministry of Defence, with a view of reinstating the Medieval lowland wet-grazing marsh to its historical glory. This area became known as Rainham Marshes.

There were grand plans for recreating the habitat to encourage a wealth of marshland species, with the dwindling lapwing and redshank being at the forefront of recovery aims. Now, just over 20 years later, the marsh is once again alive with the sound of these enigmatic wading birds. There are nearly 100 pairs of each, alongside a host of scarce breeding ducks such as gadwall, shoveler, pochard and tufted duck.

I was incredibly fortunate to be involved in the reserve from those earliest of days. Back then, you were almost as likely to see a passage hen harrier as marsh harrier quartering the fields or silt lagoons, but even then the former were on the brink.

I would see the occasional marsh harrier pushing north on a late crisp March day and hope that by the end of July we might pick up a wandering golden-crowned juvenile from further down the Thames, from the north Kent or south Essex marshes, where they had a toehold. Sometimes, one would stay for a few days and cause havoc over the pools, and one time we even had wing-tagged juveniles from the Norfolk Broads. It made you marvel at how far these young birds had already travelled – and all alone too.

It seemed as if our fledgling reed beds would never be wide enough to accommodate marsh harriers properly, and so we had to be content with watching them pass us by for many years. But then, in 2010, an immature male successfully bred in the Ingrebourne Valley, which runs north from the west end of the reserve. The adults

Altercation between a female marsh harrier and an avocet at Rainham Marshes. (© Mick Brockington)

both hunted in Rainham Marshes and the whole family spent the summer and autumn on site.

From this point onwards things changed, and visitors to Rainham Marshes now had a chance to see marsh harriers on almost any day. However, would they stay and breed with us? That was the question. A couple of years later, there were hints that it might have happened, but it wasn't until 2014 that the first Rainham brood took to the wing for sure. Each year since has seen at least one, if not two, broods raised. In 2020, while the trails were shut for Covid lockdown, three broods were seen as there was extra room for a third nest right next to the normally busy path! Our own sky dancers were nesting within the M25!

The marsh harriers here have an eclectic taste in prey and it seems that almost anything can be on the menu: they have been seen with little grebes, common gulls,

Marsh harriers flying at Rainham Marshes. (© Steve Elwell)

THE SECRET LIFE OF BIRDS OF PREY

teal, wigeon, starlings, moorhens, coots, water voles, brown rats, field voles, common lizards, grass snakes and marsh frogs, among other things. The latter are a favourite and the ditches and pools are full of them, so there is no shortage between March and October and I am sure that they are a key reason for the marsh harriers' success here. Unfortunately, the marsh harriers are also very good at taking chicks and ducklings, but as the numbers of those have also increased then the defence by those at ground level has become more vigorous.

Watching the male harrier leisurely quartering the marsh to suddenly find itself in a maelstrom of redshank, lapwing and in the last two years, deranged avocets, is a sight to behold but there must be enough food for all as both predator and prey are doing very well. Seeing any big bird of prey always raises the spirits – be it a buzzard, red kite or marsh harrier – and knowing that the marsh harriers we see on the reserve are 'ours' fills me with a warm ornithological glow.

To think that just ten years ago, breeding marsh harriers were the stuff of dreams here at Rainham Marshes, and yet you can now sit back and watch them from the comfort of the visitors' centre. With beverage in hand, you can witness the marsh harriers' low hunting style or stand outside and watch in awe as the calling male climbs high into the blue above your head, flashing black, silver and white before stooping and climbing and stooping again in his magical sky dance. It truly is a bird that makes you wish you could fly.

Where to see them

Marsh harriers are most common in east and south-east England, although some can be found in the south-west, north-west, and in Scotland.

Spy them quartering over reed beds, marshes and wetlands in search of their prey.

Good nature reserves to see them (other than Rainham Marshes in Essex) include Strumpshaw Fen in Norfolk, Wicken Fen in Cambridgeshire, Minsmere in Suffolk and Leighton Moss in Lancashire.

The marsh harrier is a rare summer visitor to Ireland, but is more likely to be seen in winter on the south-east coast. They can be seen in Wales during this time in places such as Cors Ddyga in Anglesey.

CHAPTER 8

Goshawk

Scientific name	*Accipiter gentilis*
Family	*Accipitridae* (kites, hawks and eagles)
UK conservation status	Green

'The hawk is on my fist. Thirty ounces of death in a feathered jacket.'
H is for Hawk by Helen Macdonald

History and current situation

Traditionally, the goshawk – alongside the peregrine falcon – was the preferred bird of prey for hunting through falconry. Being both fast and fearless, the goshawk is the master of stealth and ambush. It is also reliably keen for the hunt. This makes the goshawk very valuable; however, due to its fierce and destructive nature, the austringer (as keepers and trainers of goshawks were known) had to put in a lot of time, effort and dedication to successfully train the bird.

In T.H. White's diary of this process, *The Goshawk* (1951), he explains: 'The training of a goshawk ... might be expected to last about two months. In this time an ungovernable creature would have been taught to do, under government, what it would instinctively have done in two or three days in a free state.'

What White describes in this quote is how wild creatures will immediately do what is instinctive and natural to them, often guided and shown by their parents when they are very young. But taking a creature out of the wild and trying to train them to do the same things to suit us, for our own purposes, takes considerably longer. We have to earn their trust first, or bend them to our will. In his book he describes the exhausting lengths he goes to.

Even the more recent account, *H is for Hawk* (2014) by Helen Macdonald, makes it resoundingly clear that this bird is not an easy one to tame. Nevertheless, the

THE SECRET LIFE OF BIRDS OF PREY

Goshawk with jay prey. (© ondrejprosicky/Adobe Stock)

relationship she builds with her goshawk Mabel is a transformative one, helping her to heal after the death of her father.

It may be this near-untameable aspect – this true, dark wildness – combined with the powerful intensity that the goshawk possesses within its beauty that makes it so alluring. Indeed, many people such as White, Macdonald and wildlife film-maker James Aldred (see his story on page 111) are fascinated or even obsessed with the goshawk. The bird's dangerous aspect meant that, in ancient Celtic tradition, it was believed that if you uttered its name you would bring death upon your household.

Despite its proficient hunting skills, goshawk numbers in the wild have dwindled over the centuries. This is a consequence of large swathes of forests and woodlands (the goshawk's home) being cleared. The goshawk was also classed as a pest and subject to vermin lists and bounty schemes (where people were given money upon producing carcasses of said 'vermin') that simultaneously impacted most of our other birds of prey. By the late nineteenth century, the goshawk had become extinct in the UK.

From the 1960s, goshawks returned through both deliberate and accidental releases from falconries and other places, having been brought in from countries such as Poland, Germany and Finland. As a result, scattered populations established themselves in small patches, and in small numbers, across the UK. The goshawk lives secretly in these hideaways, within the depths of our extensive forests.

And yet the bird could potentially cope in smaller scraps of woodland including spinneys, overgrown graveyards and compact copses. In European cities like Berlin, there are established populations of goshawks that thrive on the urban pigeons, blackbirds and magpies to be found there, hunting on the streets and in the city's green spaces. As long as there is food available and a sturdy tree to build their big nest in, the goshawk can make it work. Perhaps with a little help and encouragement from us, this is something we could look forward to in the UK.

Currently the UK hosts around 280–430 goshawk pairs.

Unfortunately the goshawk continues to be a victim of persecution, along with nest robbery (by those who want their own goshawk).

Description, characteristics and behaviour

The goshawk looks somewhat like a sparrowhawk, except it is larger at 48–62cm in length. The male goshawk weighs in at around 600–1,100g while the female is substantially bigger at 900–2,000g. This is why this bird is known by some as the Great Hawk.

The goshawk has broad wings that are relatively short (with a wingspan of 135–165cm), a long tail, and penetrating, yellow eyes that darken with age. The male is grey on his top side and has grey horizontal stripes across his white chest. He sports a distinctive white eyebrow line that cuts across the darker plumage on his head and behind his eye.

The female is mostly brown, with brown horizontal stripes across her buff-coloured chest. She has the same white eyebrow as the male. Both have a dark grey beak that is short, hooked and savage-looking.

Juveniles are a richer, mottled brown, with vertical rather than horizontal brown stripes on their white undersides.

The shape of the goshawk's wings allows it to move at high speeds (up to 40mph) and low to the ground when hunting. The female can fly faster and more powerfully than the male; however, he is more agile and has better acceleration. He is the one that can best thread his way through and between the densely packed trees in their woodland home. This specialist ability, in this specific environment, gives the goshawk the advantage of sneaking up on its prey.

T.H. White describes this, saying that while 'falcons flew high and stooped upon their quarry [for example, kestrels]; hawks flew low and slew by stealth. Gos [the goshawk] was a chieftain among the latter.'

The elusive goshawk might begin its hunt from its favoured tree perch, where it spends most of the day hidden behind a covering of leaves. A sound may alert it to potential food, for it uses its ears as well as its eyes to detect prey.

Male goshawk eating rabbit prey. (© Erni/Adobe Stock)

Birds such as crows and pigeons and mammals such as squirrels and rabbits are on the goshawk's menu. It can catch its prey while in flight, using its long yellow legs and talons for grabbing. It occasionally goes for other birds of prey as well: kestrels, sparrowhawks, and sometimes even buzzards.

'Goshawk' comes from the combining of the words 'Goose' and 'Hawk' – a goose being its largest potential prey (although realistically this may be too large for it to tackle).

When plucking the feathers from a bird it has caught, the goshawk is very pernickety and can spend over an hour on this task. As it does so, it creates a neat ring of feathers around itself – therefore if you find this within a woodland, this could be a goshawk's food-prep spot!

Once its food is ready, the goshawk can then spend one or two hours eating. It is not one to rush a meal!

Studies have shown that the size difference between the female and male goshawk is increasing in certain areas of the UK. Where there are no longer as many woodland pheasants (the goshawk's traditional prey species), the male is decreasing in size to

Flying and screaming goshawk. (© Jan/Adobe Stock)

pursue smaller, swifter prey. Meanwhile, the female is increasing in size to better handle larger, stronger prey such as hares.

Goshawks are often at the top of the avian food chain; however, they (and especially their eggs and young) can be predated by large owls, eagles and pine martens.

The goshawk is a fairly vocal bird during the breeding season. Its calls include the throaty *gek-gek-gek* of the male responding to interlopers or predators close to the nest. Occasionally, while pursuing prey on a lengthy chase and when the victim is already aware of its presence, the goshawk may utter loud screams. Scottish novelist and poet Sir Walter Scott compared its long drawn-out cry to a shrill whistle.

Adult goshawks have an 83% year-on-year survival rate and can live to an average age of seven years in the wild. The oldest known wild goshawk, which was a ringing recovery, was almost 19 years old!

Habitat, nesting habits and breeding

The goshawk is even more secretive than the sparrowhawk to which it looks similar; it won't frequent gardens like the other will. Instead, it is faithful to large areas of open woodland or countryside such as farmland, grassland, wetland or upland, as befits its size and habits.

Goshawks are monogamous and pairs mate for life.

In late winter and early spring, the usually enigmatic bird performs a sky dance to impress its mate and maintain its territory, which it is very precious about. This takes the form of undulating dives – akin to the sparrowhawk's – consisting of deep plunges with slow-motion flapping and bullet-fast rises with wings closed tight. The male and female both take part; the female playing the key role.

The female advertises her readiness for mating with a *kek-kek-kek* vocalisation. The pair may make this sound during copulation as well.

The large and bulky goshawk nest is made from sticks and branches, lined with bark. If undisturbed, the goshawk pair will return year after year to the same general area to breed. Sometimes they even reuse the nest from the previous year. New nests are often constructed in February.

Around March time, the female lays up to four eggs over a period of around six days. These are white with a bluish tinge or dirty white in colour, occasionally patterned with brown blotches. The female incubates and protects them, and will utter a *kek-kek-kek* call to express alarm or warn intruders of her intent to mob them in defence. The male is the food provider.

After 35–38 days, the eggs hatch over two to three days. The female broods for the first ten days, after which time she will leave the nest to help with hunting, though she will remain nearby for at least 16 days – longer if the male is providing enough food.

New Forest female prepping the nest. (© James Aldred, see story on page 111)

New Forest female on her epic nest. (© James Aldred)

The goshawk chicks fledge up to 42 days after hatching. Before they fully leave the nest, however, they 'branch': spending time outside of but close to the nest, until they are strong enough to fly. They become independent when they are three months old.

Juveniles have a 40% chance of reaching their second year. They reach sexual maturity at two or three years old.

The goshawk is a resident UK bird and does not migrate.

On goshawks

Written by James Aldred, wildlife film-maker and author of Goshawk Summer: A New Forest Season Unlike Any Other *(Elliott & Thompson, 2021), which won the 2022 James Cropper Wainwright Prize for Nature Writing.*

My first experience filming goshawks in the wild was for a BBC documentary called *H is for Hawk: A New Chapter*. Working closely with Helen Macdonald (author of the original book), I had the pleasure of filming a pair of wild goshawks as they raised their brood in a quiet wood on the edge of the Forest of Dean in Gloucestershire. The year was 2016 and little by little, through countless hours of watching and filming them at their secluded nest, I felt myself being drawn irresistibly into their fascinating yet rarely seen world.

Their inherently secretive nature can make goshawks frustrating to observe, let alone film. But once in their presence, wild goshawks have a way of entering your imagination and dreams in a way that many other birds can't. I came to respect and love them in equal measure: respect them for their impressive hunting prowess, and love them for their indomitable spirit.

It's not that they're more beautiful or special than other birds of prey: they're not. It's just that for me, they seem to harbour an inner fire and focus of intent that captivates and holds attention like no other that I've filmed so far, save the harpy eagle perhaps.

I spent around 300 hours crouched with my camera in the darkness of my treetop hide that season of 2016. Highlights included witnessing the male trying to brood the eggs in his mate's absence, only to be almost killed by her when she stormed back onto the nest, and filming the female throw a full-sized rabbit down into the waiting melee of hungry mouths once her four chicks were fully grown. She didn't even land on the nest, just flew over and dropped the carcass onto their jostling heads.

At the end of the season, I remember feeling extremely privileged to have witnessed something so secretive and special. I also learned a great deal about wild goshawk behaviour from Helen and the people of the Gloucester Raptor Monitoring Group with whom we worked closely.

New Forest female feeding her three chicks. (© James Aldred)

Fast-forward four years and my next opportunity to film wild goshawks at the nest came during the spring lockdown of 2020. I jumped at the chance to re-enter the goshawks' secretive world, but what made this opportunity particularly enticing for me was that it was to be based within the New Forest National Park.

I grew up in the New Forest, but back then in the 1980s–90s, the thought of it once again being home to wild goshawks was a mere fantasy. Persecution had removed them from the Forest some 150 years earlier. It is only recently, within the past 20 years, that they have begun to show up again and returned to breed there. So it was another privileged experience for me, heightened further by having permission to film within the forest during one of the strangest periods in recent history.

Again, I spent over 300 hours observing and filming the daily life in the nest; again, from a treetop filming hide that I installed 50ft off the ground in a tree adjacent to the nest. And once again I relied heavily on local expertise, in this case kindly provided by the Forestry Commission, and the local forest keepers in particular.

What amazed me most about this particular nest was just how different the two adult birds were in their behaviour to those in the Forest of Dean. Whereas the male and female in 2016 spent very little time in each other's company – indeed seemed to shun each other, and even display aggression – the New Forest pair seemed a lot more relaxed and cohesive. The Hampshire female even tolerated the male's clumsy attempts to help incubate the eggs and newly hatched chicks, only nudging him gently away when he was in danger of damaging the brood.

It also became evident that the Hampshire male was a lot older than the female, and probably from a different genetic heritage. Whereas she was a hulking brown bird of immense size and power, who probably carried DNA from escaped falconry birds originally imported from Germany, he was of Nordic origin – a fact clearly suggested by his crisp grey and silver plumage. His eyes were a lot darker than hers too. She had beautiful irises of deep yellow, but his were blood red. Like rubies; truly magical and mysterious. This is a trait that normally suggests an older bird.

So, we seemed to have a younger hawk of Germanic ancestry coupled with a much older tiercel carrying genes from Sweden or Finland.

The couple successfully raised three chicks during lockdown that season: two females and one smaller, flighty male. All three were gone from the nest by 26 June.

I returned to the breeding site the following spring to see if the adults intended to raise another brood there again. Compared to six months before – at the end of the previous summer – when the nest had appeared noticeably tired and in need of repair, it was now newly fluffed up with fresh twigs and foliage. A clear sign that another breeding season had started.

On this occasion I also caught a glimpse of the female perched high in a fir tree on the ridge above the nest site. She was watching me. Perhaps she even recognised me. But, as fond as I am of these birds, the most I could ever wish for in return is to be tolerated. After all, sentimentality is not part of a goshawk's natural demeanour.

New Forest female with her three chicks, who are close to fledging. (© James Aldred)

Where to see them

The highest numbers of goshawks are found in south Scotland and in Wales; they are mostly absent – except for small patches – from the rest of the UK.

The best time to see goshawks is when they are performing their display flights over the trees on a clear day in late winter and early spring.

If you are lucky you might spot them hunting over open countryside, or even luckier, along woodland and forest paths and glades. Try RSPB Nag's Head and places including the New Forest in Hampshire and the Forest of Dean in Gloucestershire. Guided tours for beginners are available in North Yorkshire.

The absence of corvid nests can be a sign of a goshawk's habitat, as the corvids are understandably not keen to nest close to one of their predators! And if you hear the raucous sound of agitated corvids, this could be their alarm call indicating the presence of a goshawk.

Goshawk clashing with a buzzard. (© Piotr Krzeslak/Adobe Stock)

CHAPTER 9

Sparrowhawk

Scientific name	*Accipiter nisus*
Family	*Accipitridae* (kites, hawks and eagles)
UK conservation status	Amber

'Those eyes in their helmet ... they alone/Laser the
lark-shaped hole/In the lark's song.'

A Sparrow-Hawk by Ted Hughes

History and current situation

In falconry, the male sparrowhawk is referred to as a musket, which is where the name for the early gun used by infantry was derived.

Destruction and removal of woodlands has reduced the amount of suitable habitat available for the sparrowhawk, thereby leading to an inevitable decline in numbers. And yet numbers were fairly stable (due to a natural balance between the sparrowhawk and its prey) until gamekeepers discriminated against it from the 1800s. It was also targeted by trophy hunters from this time.

Studies show that this species only takes a small percentage of game birds as part of its diet and therefore it is not as much of a threat as some perceive it to be.

It was in the 1840s that the sparrowhawk was first given legal protection. However, this did not completely stop the practice of shooting and poisoning. Luckily, and unlike several other bird of prey species, the sparrowhawk managed to avoid extinction, possibly due to its ability to keep itself hidden from us.

Fewer illegal kills during the Second World War allowed the sparrowhawk's numbers to increase. But by the 1950s, it had to contend with the impact of pesticides, including DDT, instead. These agricultural poisons worked their way up the food chain, to the point where many sparrowhawk eggshells were too thin for chick development and hatching to be successful. The sparrowhawk population across the

Male sparrowhawk. (© Sandi Monger, see story on page 123)

UK crashed as a result, and it became almost extinct in the east of England where the pesticides were most heavily used.

After many of the toxic chemicals were banned, the sparrowhawk population grew once more, although it wasn't until the 1980s that the eastern populations began to breed successfully.

Contaminants can still be found (in residual amounts) within these birds today; thankfully it no longer depresses their numbers. In 1963 the sparrowhawk also became a fully legally protected bird.

In 1990, there were an estimated 32,000 breeding pairs in the UK. This number has since risen to an estimated 35,000 breeding pairs. Though this is an excellent number, the decline of smaller bird species and areas of suitable habitat limits (and sometimes reduces) sparrowhawk numbers.

Certain people believe that the sparrowhawk negatively impacts the amount of smaller bird species; however, long-term scientific studies prove that it has little to no impact on songbird populations. Food chains work in balance, with species living alongside each other for thousands of years without such problems. There will never be enough sparrowhawks in one place to decimate songbird numbers, as the number of suitable nest sites and food availability naturally restricts how many an area can host.

The sparrowhawk itself does not have many predators, being often at the top of the food chain where it lives. However, sparrowhawk chicks and fledglings can be taken by goshawks or pine martens. They can also be vulnerable to large owls, eagles and peregrine falcons.

Its place in the food chain makes the sparrowhawk a useful indicator of the overall health of an ecosystem: the ecosystem is healthier when the bird is present.

Description, characteristics and behaviour

The sparrowhawk is a relatively small bird of prey; yet, when you see one you will agree that there is a presence about it, and that it is imbued with a nervous tension, ready to disappear at any moment.

The female sparrowhawk is brown on her upper side, with brown horizontal bars across her white chest and belly. The male meanwhile is blue-grey on his upper side (he is known as the Blue Hawk in counties such as Berkshire), with orange-brown horizontal bars. Both have a long tail, grey beaks, yellow legs and long, deadly talons.

The adults' eyes are yellow or orange, sometimes almost red, with large black pupils that give them a sinister look. Young sparrowhawks' eyes are greenish yellow.

As with most other birds of prey, the female is larger than the male. She is around 185–342g in weight, while the male is 110–196g. This means that the female is nearly twice the weight of the male – this is called reversed sexual size dimorphism, and it is particularly noticeable in the sparrowhawk pair. The male needs to be small and light for his high-speed chases (see below), whereas the female can afford to be larger as she hunts less and needs the extra fat reserves to produce and incubate her eggs, and to defend the nest.

The length of a sparrowhawk ranges from 28–38cm (it is smaller than a wood pigeon) and the span of its short, rounded wings is 55–70cm. It has a distinctive flap-flap-glide flight pattern that can help you to distinguish the sparrowhawk from other birds of prey.

Due to the size difference, the female can catch prey up to the size of a pigeon, whereas the male catches birds up to the size of a thrush. Both hunt sparrows (the clue is in the name) and they have been known to catch bats and other mammals too.

The sparrowhawk hunting technique is to approach its prey surreptitiously, lurking among the trees or flying low behind cover while it chooses its victim. When the perfect opportunity arises, it swoops in with a burst of speed to make the kill. Not built for stamina or long chases, the sparrowhawk is instead able to manoeuvre more efficiently when in pursuit (using an agile, twisting flight) than other birds of prey. Its flying speed averages 30–40kph, although it can reach up to 50kph in short bursts.

Female sparrowhawk. (© Sandi Monger, see story on page 123)

Male sparrowhawk in a snowy woodland. (© Chloé Valerie Harmsworth)

The sparrowhawk eats any species of bird within the size range it can catch, and in summer 40% of its diet is made up of fledglings. It grabs its prey with its very long toes and talons and takes it away to pluck and eat. Unfortunately, the victim isn't always dead when it's being de-feathered!

Another technique that the sparrowhawk can employ is drowning its prey, which it tends to do with larger birds such as magpies.

The sparrowhawk, in ideal conditions, can live up to seven years, although this is rare. The average lifespan is around 2.7 years. Annually, around a third of adults die – usually in March and April when food supply is at its lowest – and only two thirds of sparrowhawk fledglings survive their first year.

The primary cause of death is starvation. Food availability also impacts the number of young produced by a breeding pair, and just under half of all sparrowhawk nests produce no young during the breeding season. Prolonged winter weather is a factor in how soon and how successfully the adults breed.

A mostly silent bird, the sparrowhawk may sometimes make a variety of noises, especially around the breeding season. One of its most common calls is a *kewkewkewkew* or *kekekeke*.

Habitat, nesting habits and breeding

Due to its compact size and ability to hunt birds in confined spaces, the sparrowhawk is able to remain under the cover of woodlands. However, these features also allow it to search for prey in gardens – such as small birds around bird feeders. This means the sparrowhawk can be found not just in rural environments but urban ones too. Due to this flexibility, this bird can be found across the UK, except for parts of the Western Isles, Shetland and the Scottish Highlands.

Early in the year and during spring, sparrowhawks leave the safety of their woodland to perform roller coaster display flights high in the sky above it. They gain height with slow flaps of their wings before taking a dive. They repeat this again and again, re-establishing their ownership of the territory. Somewhat surprisingly, the female may take the lead on this, the male occasionally following her flight path. This forms part of their courtship before the breeding season begins.

Flying female sparrowhawk. (© Andrew Steele)

Above left and above right: *Sparrowhawk as a chick and juvenile. (© Sandi Monger, see story on page 123)*

Sparrowhawks refuse to share territories with other birds of their species and therefore the distance between nests depends on the availability of food in the area. If supply is plentiful, they can exist relatively close together; if not, a larger range is observed. The average distance between nests ranges from 0.5km to 2.1km.

The ideal nest spot is fairly low down and close to the trunk of a tree, hidden from prying eyes. On occasion sparrowhawks will nest on a cliff edge. They prefer to use an abandoned squirrel drey or another bird's old nest as a base for theirs.

The nest is a sturdy but untidy flattish construction of twigs, lined with softer materials such as down or bark fibres, with a central cup to hold the eggs. Nest building, which takes several weeks, is completed long before eggs are laid.

Sparrowhawks align their egg laying with the time when smaller birds, for example those of the tit species, are ready to fledge: easy-to-catch fledglings are the perfect food source for their own newborns.

During May, the female lays up to six white eggs – that may be tinged with green or blue and have reddish brown markings interspersed with purple blotches – at two-day intervals. She incubates these for up to 35 days, after which they hatch at similar intervals. This successive hatching allows for an unpredictable food supply: if supplies are limited, the youngest will die so that the brood size matches supplies.

Newborn sparrowhawks are born covered in white down, with their eyes partially open. The female helps them to break out of their shell. She broods her young constantly during the first week, and less as time goes on, until they can regulate their own body temperatures. Meanwhile, the male provides the female and young with food. Later on, if the male needs help catching sufficient food for the growing chicks, the female will join the hunt.

Young sparrowhawk with a starling in a garden. (© Barry Madden)

When the young sparrowhawks fledge (at around four weeks), they initially only leave the nest for short periods and return to it to eat and sleep. As the weeks pass, they become braver and more independent of the nest and their parents. They spend a month (usually July) learning essential skills by watching their parents hunt, and by practising their own hunting techniques. Gradually, the inexperienced sparrowhawks develop the ability to feed themselves, until they no longer need their parents' help or intervention. They are now ready to go it alone as young adults, dispersing from the area to establish their own territories.

Being a year-round UK resident, the sparrowhawk does not migrate in autumn. Instead, it feasts on the flying buffets that are around at this time of year: flocks of small, foraging birds. It does this by selecting and picking off the vulnerable individuals at the edge of the flock – those who have been pushed to the outside by dominant birds in the centre.

This doesn't always work; sometimes flocks of birds mob their predator at the predator's roost site, perches or even while in flight, in an attempt to move the danger on. Although the strategy of crowding the predator while flicking their tails and wings and sounding alarm calls is very risky, it can be successful – perhaps because the predator becomes confused or annoyed and doesn't want the hassle!

It has been suggested that the sparrowhawk may have contributed to the decrease in song thrush numbers – probably because it hunts them year round.

Come depths-of-winter January, all bets are off, and the female sparrowhawk will even resort to hunting and eating smaller male sparrowhawks to assuage her desperate hunger.

The sparrowhawk family
Written by Sandi Monger from Norwich, Norfolk, who works in retail and volunteers with the RSPB.

I've always loved animals, but I'm not one of those who can say 'I've known since I was little that I wanted to work with wildlife', because that's not the case. When I left school at 15, I hit a really low point and had no idea what I wanted in life. Then I realised that wildlife was my constant happiness, so I went to college and studied Animal Management. I loved it so much that I then went and got a first-class degree in Animal Behaviour! I've volunteered and done research in the UK, Tenerife and South Africa, but I will always have a big love for UK birds of prey – especially sparrowhawks.

In 2021, I was super lucky in terms of seeing and spending time with birds of prey. While on nature walks I would see buzzards, kestrels and sometimes red kites, but I never saw sparrowhawks. Towards the end of March I spotted a pair of tawny owls with three owlets, which was amazing, and being on furlough I got to visit them regularly. They were situated in a tiny woodland with a small path next to it. This path was surrounded by vegetation, and next to a stream and the River Wensum. Between the stream and the river was a fallen tree on which I would often rest. One day, while watching the owls, a sparrowhawk flew past me very low and landed on a nearby branch. It was my first proper encounter; I thought it was incredible. A burst of adrenaline shot through my veins and I felt so excited.

I waited on the same log the next day, in the hope that it would come back. My patience and determination was rewarded when I noticed a sparrowhawk sitting on the other side of the river. I got up and walked over to photograph it. After 15 minutes it flew further downriver to a different tree and I followed it. I was with it for a further 45 minutes. How rare to spend this amount of time with a wild animal. When I got

Female sparrowhawk. (@ Sandi Monger)

home and looked at my photographs, I noticed that I had actually seen both the male and female sparrowhawk – a total surprise to me. My optimistic self then started thinking 'a pair: they must be nesting' and 'imagine if they're nesting nearby' and more excitement started to brew within me.

Pretty much every day after that I managed to observe both the male and female doing aerial displays, nest building, mating, food passes, incubating eggs, raising chicks, and I watched the chicks fledge. My favourite part was seeing the chicks grow from tiny white balls to adult-looking birds (see photos on page 121). I felt as though these birds were mine, as if I was part of the family. I wasn't, of course. These birds did not care about me, but I cared about them a lot.

Sparrowhawks are now very special to me because previously I rarely saw them and I was constantly jealous of other people's experiences. With sparrowhawks being moved from IUCN's Green List to the Amber List in 2021, it feels especially amazing to have witnessed a pair raise and fledge four chicks. Months after the chicks fledged, I saw one hunting in the area successfully and it warmed my heart to know that they're still about and doing well.

Male sparrowhawk. (© Sandi Monger)

I've recently heard a sparrowhawk in a woodland not far from the pair. I wonder if it's one of the fledglings now pairing and mating? How wonderful that would be! Indeed, as well as the original pair's nest, I have found two other nest sites this year (at the time of writing in spring 2022), so I'll be keeping my eye on those!

Getting a glimpse into the sparrowhawks' lives has been truly unforgettable, and I feel incredibly lucky.

Where to see them

Sparrowhawks are found across the UK except in parts of the Western Isles, Shetland and the Scottish Highlands.

They are one of the most common resident birds of prey in Ireland. They can be seen throughout the country, although numbers are lower in parts of the west, where tree cover is low.

Sparrowhawks are enigmatic birds, preferring to stay out of sight. However, you may chance upon one hunting or sitting on a branch within a woodland.

In your garden, the sudden scattering of birds from feeders or sharp alarm calls may alert you to the presence of a sparrowhawk. If they catch something, they may even stay in your garden to pluck the feathers from it.

Example RSPB reserves that you can try include Blean Woods in Kent, Blowers Marsh in Essex and Wolves Wood in Suffolk.

CHAPTER 10

White-tailed eagle

Scientific name	*Haliaeetus albicilla*
Family	*Accipitridae* (kites, hawks and eagles)
UK conservation status	Amber

Iolaire sùil na grèine – 'eagle of the sunlit eye'
(A Gaelic name for the white-tailed eagle)

History and current situation

The first part of the white-tailed eagle's scientific name, *Haliaeetus*, comes from the Greek word *halos* meaning 'the sea', and *aetos* for 'eagle' – referring to its other common name of sea eagle. The second part, *albicilla*, comes from the Latin words *albus* for 'white' and *cilla* for 'tail'.

The white-tailed eagle was common in the UK until its numbers started to decrease in the early nineteenth century. Up to this point the bird had been widespread in Scotland and Ireland, and bred in England as well. Over 50 eyries (nests) were known of in Ireland and over 100 existed in Britain.

The illegal killing of this eagle by gamekeepers, fishery owners and shepherds (usually by lacing carrion with poison or by shooting the bird), meant that it became extinct in the UK during the early twentieth century. Egg collectors and skin collectors also played their part in this magnificent bird's downfall.

By 1800, the white-tailed eagle had disappeared from England, though it lasted a little longer in Ireland, until eventually there were just a few pairs remaining in the UK – in Scotland. The last record of white-tailed eagle breeding on the Isle of Skye was in 1916 and the last Scottish individual was shot in Shetland in 1918. It had been completely wiped out.

To bring it back to the UK, conservationists reintroduced white-tailed eagles sourced from Norway – and it is from these birds that our current population is

White-tailed eagle on hare prey. (© mzphoto11/Adobe Stock)

descended. The programme, run by the Nature Conservancy Council (now known as NatureScot) and the RSPB, began in 1975 and released 82 white-tailed eagles on the Isle of Rum over ten years.

Following this, the first successful white-tailed eagle breeding was recorded on the Isle of Mull in 1985. Since then, more and more pairs have nested successfully there. From 1993 to 1998, more were released in Wester Moss, and from 2007 to 2012, in Fife. As a result of these efforts, the white-tailed eagle population in Scotland has become self-sustaining, and therefore chicks from this population are being used to reintroduce the bird back to England, in places such as the Isle of Wight. In 2019, for example, six young Scottish birds were released there by Forestry England working alongside the Roy Dennis Wildlife Foundation.

Unfortunately, pesticides reduced white-tailed eagle breeding success into the 1980s. DDT and polychlorinated biphenyls (PCBs) have been recorded in eagle eggs; it is believed that this comes from the fulmars that the white-tailed eagle sometimes predates.

Furthermore, the white-tailed eagle is affected by poisoned carrion – either intentionally by people targeting eagles, or accidentally. In the latter case, the dead animal may have ingested a poison left for it (for example if it is a 'pest' such as a fox

White-tailed eagle going in for a catch. (© Donna Robinson)

or crow) or inadvertently consumed toxins found in its environment (polluted water, sprayed plants etc.).

Humans who deliberately aim to kill the eagle are usually acting in the belief that it predates animal stock. However, although this can occur, studies show low levels of lamb predation by eagles, with few incidents ever witnessed. Conservationists therefore try to work with landowners, livestock producers and workers to resolve these concerns and issues – for example, by implementing scaring devices and providing diversionary feeding for the eagles. Payment is also given to farmers by the Sea Eagle Management Scheme to encourage positive management.

Sadly, instances of nest robbing and illegal disturbances still occur. Larger fines have been implemented as a deterrent, but the surveillance and protection of white-tailed eagle nests remains essential and necessary.

Another important factor is the white-tailed eagle's habitat. Although this can be problematic due to the bird's extensive flight range over both private and open land, general land use policies exist to ensure places remain appropriate for nesting and feeding. The monitoring of eagles through ringing programmes, satellite tracking, field surveys and so forth provides conservationists with data on the bird's range and habits, giving information on how the white-tailed eagle can be helped further.

Finally, like other large birds of prey, the white-tailed eagle is slower to breed: it takes around five years to reach breeding age; rearing their young takes longer; only one or two chicks are reared each year. Because of this, the population of white-tailed eagles does not grow as quickly as those of smaller and faster-living birds of prey.

In 2020, there were an estimated 150 breeding pairs in the UK. It is believed that by 2025 there could be over 200.

The white-tailed eagle is boosting local economies in places like Mull and Skye through eco-tourism. This is great, but we must take care not to disturb these birds and we should respect their environment too. (See more on pages 19–20.)

Description, characteristics and behaviour

Larger than the golden eagle, the white-tailed eagle is the largest bird of prey in the UK, at 70–90cm in length. The male weighs 3.5–5kg and the female is larger at 4–7kg.

The white-tailed eagle has a brown body, a paler neck and head, and white tail feathers (hence the name). Its tail is short and wedge-shaped and its massive wings are long and broad, with long finger-shaped primary feathers at their ends. Its epic wingspan of 200–240cm is the reason it is called the 'flying barn door'. It has yellow legs and a chunky, hooked yellow beak. Its eyes are pale with a large black pupil, rimmed with yellow.

White-tailed eagle with fish. (© Donna Robinson)

Juveniles are a darker black-brown in colour. They gain their adult plumage at five or six years, but their tail does not turn white until they are eight years old.

The white-tailed eagle often flies following the shoreline, moving fast despite its slow, shallow wingbeats. It can be seen circling an area in wide arcs and using thermals to help it gain height, from which it can glide downwards to its destination using minimal effort and energy.

The white-tailed eagle feeds on a variety of things such as rabbits, hares and various birds, as it is both an opportunistic hunter and a carrion feeder. Examples of carrion include dead deer and lambs.

Since fish forms the majority of its diet, it is also known as the sea eagle. It sources fish by flying then hovering low over water before reaching forward with its legs to snatch one from the surface. The spiked texture on the soles of its feet helps it to grip this slippery food. Shetland fishermen so respected the bird's fishing prowess that they anointed bait with the bird's fat to bring them luck and success in their own fishing endeavours.

The white-tailed eagle also steals fish from otters and birds including gulls and osprey, chasing them until they drop their catch. In return, when it catches a fish, the eagle can be mobbed by gulls, though the gulls rarely succeed in taking the fish.

The white-tailed eagle, as an apex predator, has no natural predators of its own. It has a plaintive, yelping cry.

Its average life span is 21 years. Some live longer, however, and the oldest recorded individual was around 32 years old!

Habitat, nesting habits and breeding

The white-tailed eagle can be found in marine, intertidal and wetland habitats, as well as on farmland and uplands.

While still relatively scarce in the UK, most breeding white-tailed eagles can be found on Scotland's north and west coasts and nearby islands (the Isle of Mull has the highest density of breeding white-tailed eagles in Scotland).

Reintroduction programmes are currently working towards bringing the bird back to Scotland's east coast, Ireland and England's Isle of Wight. This means that there is a (albeit small) possibility of seeing one flying overhead wherever you live – but especially close to the areas mentioned – as individuals spread out and explore.

Although generally found in remote, rural areas, the white-tailed eagle is able to adapt to more populated areas too. When supported by various organisations, it can nest in commercial forestry plantations.

Breeding pairs are monogamous and usually pair for life, unless one dies. This would most likely be the male, as a result of a territorial dispute with another white-tailed eagle.

White-tailed eagle fighting with a golden eagle. (© Johannes Jensås/Adobe Stock)

White-tailed eagles can live comfortably side-by-side with golden eagles, despite some competition for food – usually over carrion in winter. The golden eagle has dominance here, even though it is the smaller of the two. This is because it is the stronger flier, frequently winning aerial conflicts. Thankfully, the white-tailed eagle can survive on less food.

White-tailed eagles tend to nest in trees, while golden eagles go for cliff edges. However, if nest sites are limited – say because of deforestation and degraded habitats – this can cause further competition between the two species. In this war, the white-tailed eagle will most likely be the victor.

At the beginning of the year, the breeding pair of white-tailed eagles calls loudly to one another close to their nest (known as an eyrie). They strengthen their bond by flying together in aerial displays of circles, loops, tumbles and rolls, occasionally duetting and touching talons.

White-tailed eagles can be witnessed locking claws mid-air, cartwheeling downwards and separating at the last moment, shockingly close to the ground or water beneath them, before soaring back up. It is thought that this occurs when one of the pair is defending its territory against an intruder.

White-tailed eagle chicks in nest. (© predrag1/Adobe Stock)

The eyrie is built from branches and twigs, lined with grass and rushes. Nests are used for years, with new material added each time. For this reason, eyries can reach an incredible size. New nests may be built following an unsuccessful year of breeding.

In March or April, the female lays up to three dull white eggs two to five days apart. Each egg is incubated for 38 days, almost exclusively by the female. The chicks hatch from their shells a few days apart and are tolerant of each other, though the oldest is the dominant one.

The brooding and feeding is carried out mostly by the female, with the male taking over for short periods. During the first few weeks, the male brings in food for the female and their young. After this, the female joins in with the hunting. At the age of five to six weeks, the chicks feed themselves with what the parents bring to the nest.

When they are ten to 11 weeks old, the chicks are ready to fledge. Yet, for another six weeks or so, they remain nearby – they are still dependent on their parents for food and to learn the skills they need to survive on their own.

White-tailed eagle landing on nest with food for its juvenile chicks. (© Daniel Dunca/Adobe Stock)

Juveniles often remain close to their nesting area, sometimes gathering in groups of up to ten individuals. Young birds usually pair up and breed at around five years old, once they have established a permanent home range.

White-tailed eagles do not migrate and so can be seen in the UK year round.

The sight of sea eagles
Written by Chloé Valerie Harmsworth.

Our cottage boasted a huge window overlooking the shining water of the Sound of Mull. Beyond this colour-changing glossiness – that reflected the weather and time of day – lay the other side of the bay, with its row of custodian conifers.

With high season over, Mull was quiet. But we were full of excitement. Amy, her parents and I each had a list of the species we wanted to see, and at the top of all of them were eagles.

It might be known as Eagle Island, yet the breeding season (when eagle parents tend to their young and hunt more frequently, affording numerous spotting opportunities), was also done with. So would we get anything more than just a fleeting flash of one?

On the day we arrived we drove to Loch na Keal, hoping to see sea eagles. We appreciated an otter swimming and diving for food, as well as the soulful sound of curlews, but saw no eagles. Standing in the bone-drenching rain, I couldn't blame them for sheltering out of sight. We consoled ourselves that evening with a takeaway by the fire.

The weather wasn't much better the next morning and yet, ever hopeful, we drove into the mountains. On the journey, eagle-eyed Amy spotted the eerie silhouette of a vast bird soaring into the sombre clouds of a high peak; that afternoon while consuming cake and tea, we saw two (probably golden eagles) flying over a distant mountain. Although frustrating, these tantalising glimpses ensured we would really appreciate a better view ...

... which we got the next day! After breakfast, as I packed my bag, I heard the long-awaited yell of 'Eagle!' coming from the living room. I ran in to see my fellow nature obsessives' binoculars trained on the conifers. Grabbing mine, I pointed them towards the second tree from the left. There, on the second branch from the top, sat a sea eagle!

Facing away from us, he preened – arching his neck round to access the hard-to-reach feathers on his back, then addressing his armpits and wings. Bending forwards to his chest and belly, he perfectly displayed his bright white tail feathers. In our magnified circles, the backdrop of sandy-green mountains was touched by gentle sunlight that illuminated his hefty yellow beak. He turned around, allowing us to admire his noble face and lemony legs, before flying away. We released a communal sigh as what we had seen sunk in.

He returned the next morning, sitting on the same branch of the same tree. But he wasn't alone. Below him sat another, larger, sea eagle – the female. We regarded them through the misty air and Dave's scope before reluctantly departing (we had a boat to catch).

The peace on Mull meant we were the sole viewers at most viewing points. The exception came when, two days later, we visited Loch na Keal again. Pairs, individuals and groups of other wildlife lovers joined us, the cameras getting bigger each time, until the place was at full capacity. The atmosphere was akin to an audience anticipating the arrival of their favourite performer.

After two hours, Rose spotted a sea eagle on the wing. It landed in a tree on the ridge behind us, its face obscured by a branch. A second flew in and landed seven trees away from the first, but in a prominent 'look at me' position. She was a mocha-coloured female, with a necklace of paler, shortbread-hued feathers around

THE SECRET LIFE OF BIRDS OF PREY

Sitting white-tailed eagles. (© Karen Blow)

her throat. These ruffled in the breeze as she surveyed her kingdom (or should I say queendom?), her strength clear in the grip of her talons.

At one point she cried out to the male with a surprisingly sharp, yelping puppy-like call. It rang through the silent air, bounced off the landscape and the loch, and startled us with its surround-sound effect. She then flew a lap above us and over part of the loch, before landing on another tree.

We watched the pair for four hours. By the time we were suffering acutely from bird-neck and binocular-back, as well as mental over-stimulation ('fateagled', as Amy described it), the female had adjourned to a rocky outcrop on the mountain. The male, meanwhile, had moved to a patch of grass and was pecking, chicken-style, possibly at some food.

The highlight for me was seeing the female ensconced in a clump of bracken, her head poking out comically and glowing gloriously against the emerald and bronze vegetation.

Flying white-tailed eagle. (© Karen Blow)

Unable to take any more of this magnificence, and thoroughly in need of nourishment, we sojourned to Salen to recuperate. We had achieved our mission and it was time to celebrate.

Mull had given us what we dreamed of. We needed nothing else. And yet, its generosity continued. The following morning, sitting by the window with a hangover almost as epic as the island's wildlife, I somehow espied a shape above the water. 'Eagle!!!'

Our team called to attention, the sea eagle swept the sky in rings, coming ever closer. Amy and I hastened outside in bare feet and PJs, to see it soar over us and the cottage. This farewell, on our last full day, bestowed upon us our best view of those spectacular barn doors. We looked up in awe and absolute gratitude.

Where to see them

You can see white-tailed eagles in the places and regions mentioned in the habitat section of this chapter, and at RSPB reserves such as Loch Druidibeg in Scotland.

Look for it perched on a tree or rock beside the shoreline or loch, where it spends much of its time (another of its Gaelic names is *Iolaire Chladaich*, the Shore Eagle). Look for a big bird, but note that its colouring can provide excellent camouflage against its background!

What is particularly noticeable about the bird's silhouette in flight is its long and thick protruding neck, its large wings and bulky beak. You can truly appreciate its dimensions when you see it flying alongside other birds (for example gulls or corvids that may be dive-bombing it – a regular occurrence). You can also witness a speed and agility that is surprising for its size. The flashing white of its tail will help you to spot it in the air.

On the island of South Ronaldsay in the archipelago of Orkney is 'The Tomb of the Eagles'. Discovered in 1958 by farmer Ronnie Simison, it is a Neolithic chambered cairn that overlooks Isbister's cliffs. Inside the tomb human remains, tools, and the bones of 35 birds of prey – two thirds of these white-tailed eagles – were found. There were 70 white-tailed eagle talons in total, some of these buried beside the human skeletons.

We can therefore reasonably assume that the white-tailed eagle was of great significance to this Neolithic community, and that shamanistic rituals might have been carried out for the dead: the eagles potentially guiding them on their journey to the afterlife. Indeed, eagles and other birds have been used by various cultures across the world in similar ceremonies.

Flying white-tailed eagle. (© Daniel/Adobe Stock)

The weathering and damage to the human bones suggests that they may have been exposed to the elements for a while before burial. One theory is that they were left to be picked clean by carrion eaters, including white-tailed eagles, before being moved underground. Did the people perhaps believe that, as the flesh was eaten, the human soul was transferred to live on in the bird?

The tomb is closed for 2022–23 but may reopen in the future.

CHAPTER 11

Golden eagle

Scientific name	*Aquila chrysaetos*
Family	*Accipitridae* (kites, hawks and eagles)
UK conservation status	Green

'He clasps the crag with crooked hands;
Close to the sun in lonely lands,
Ring'd with the azure world, he stands.'

The Eagle by Alfred, Lord Tennyson

History and current situation

Aquila comes from the Latin *aquilus*, meaning 'dark-coloured' or 'brownish', and *chrysaetos* comes from the Ancient Greek *khrusos*, meaning 'gold', and *aetos*, meaning 'eagle'.

Many countries and cultures revere the golden eagle, and it appears on coats of arms and flags. It is the national bird of Germany and Mexico and, although the osprey is giving it a run for its money, many people consider the golden eagle to be the symbol of Scotland.

The bird's bulky form, broad wings and impressive size ooze strength and power. There's something mysterious and magical about it, which is why it is repeatedly used as a spiritual symbol (eagle gods, for example). The eagle was the sacred animal companion and messenger of Zeus, the topmost of the Greek gods.

The Roman legions carried standards (spears with various symbols on them) that featured the aquila – a golden eagle. The man who carried it was called the aquilifer.

This majestic bird is often featured on the front of church lecterns, the stand from which the Bible is read to parishioners. This may be because the eagle – one of the four beasts of Revelations – is assigned to the apostle St John, the bearer of the Word.

Golden eagle with prey. (© Jesus/Adobe Stock)

Our phrases such as 'eagle-eyed', 'swift as an eagle' and 'fierce as an eagle' show our respect for this bird's amazing eyesight, power and speed. Indeed, eagle feathers were added to arrows in the belief that they would make them fly faster.

As with other birds of prey, the golden eagle has been and sometimes still is victimised by humans: killed, poisoned, and its eggs stolen.

It was in the eighteenth century when the population of golden eagles began to decline in the UK. The perpetrators were sheep farmers, who thought they were protecting their flocks from predation; the killing was continued by gamekeepers in the nineteenth century. By 1850, the golden eagle was extinct in England and Wales and, by 1912, in Ireland as well. Thankfully, small numbers survived in Scotland, although life wasn't easy for these few.

Changes in land use and the practice of using organochlorine pesticides in agriculture impacted the remaining golden eagle population. The latter moved up the food chain to become concentrated in these birds' bodies, leading to infertility or eggshell thinning (and therefore unsuccessful broods).

After many deadly pesticides were banned, the Scottish golden eagle population slowly recovered. And yet large areas of the golden eagle's former range are still to be reclaimed. According to recent studies, illegal persecution (particularly on grouse moors in the central and eastern Highlands) and low food availability (especially in the western Highlands) act as constraints that prevent the size and range of the current golden eagle population from increasing.

In many areas land has been overgrazed by livestock and deer – with heather and other plants being stripped away, the environment has become lower quality as a result. It supports less wildlife, so the live prey that the golden eagle depends upon are not abundant. This lack means that golden eagle numbers cannot increase: the nutritional value of live prey (rather than carrion) is essential for a golden eagle to breed. Conservation organisations are making it a priority to resolve these issues by tackling persecution and changing the management of deer and sheep to promote food availability.

One golden eagle pair has bred in the Lake District in recent years. However, although juveniles range far and wide in their exploratory flights, none have colonised appropriate sites in south-east Scotland (there are a handful of pairs in south-west Scotland) and northern England yet. This could be down to persecution or disturbance in these places. With a little help though, perhaps they will one day.

There are currently around 440 breeding golden eagle pairs in the UK.

Description, characteristics and behaviour

The golden eagle is a huge bird of prey at 75–88cm in length. It is mostly warm brown in colour, with a golden head and neck. It has lighter patches on the underside of its wings and black on the tips of its feathers. It has yellow legs and a chunky, hooked yellow and black beak. The male weighs around 2.8–4.5kg and the female weighs between 3.8–6.6kg.

Golden eagle pair. (© Paolo/Adobe Stock)

The golden eagle's broad wings reach a wingspan of 204–220cm. It also has a long, fan-shaped tail.

Juveniles have more individual white and black feathers (for example, obvious white patches on the underside of their wings), and less brown than the adults.

The white-tailed eagle is the only bird of prey larger than the golden eagle in the UK.

In the sky, the golden eagle's silhouette has been mistaken for the buzzard, but the golden eagle is a much larger bird. In fact, the buzzard has jokingly been called the 'tourists' eagle' by people living in Scotland, due to visitors frequently misidentifying buzzards as golden eagles. The golden eagle's more pronounced 'fingers' at its wing tips can help to differentiate it from the buzzard.

The golden eagle's flight patterns include soaring and gliding on air currents, with its wings held in a shallow 'V'. It can cope with strong winds, flying easily into headwinds, and hold itself motionless in conditions in which a human would struggle to stand upright! This adds to the popular concept of the eagle symbolising strength, power and perseverance.

The golden eagle eats most birds and mammals that are available to it. Those that hunt over moorlands and mountains have a diet consisting mainly of young deer, hares, rabbits, foxes, ptarmigan and grouse. The golden eagle of the coast hunts for seabirds, including gulls.

Golden eagle on carrion in winter. (© Wirestock Creators/Adobe Stock)

When hunting over land, the golden eagle flies low and, with a quick rush, strikes with its talons. It does not usually dive for prey from a great height, but when it does, it folds its wings in and descends in a fast, angled glide. It uses this technique as it relies on a surprise attack – it rarely succeeds in long chases.

It takes birds such as grouse on the wing, although it needs to have built up enough momentum to be successful, since grouse fly fast. Luckily the golden eagle's brown colouring can help it to blend in with a hillside or mountain (except when there's snow), providing a useful camouflage that makes it harder for prey to spot it coming.

Golden eagle pairs may hunt together, but it is unusual to find a group of golden eagles together at a single site sourcing food. One reason for this is that, as an apex predator, the golden eagle does not need safety in numbers.

Carrion provides the bird with larger items such as adult deer. This is especially important in winter, when other food sources might be scarce. After indulging in a large meal, a golden eagle may not need to eat again for days.

Large prey needs to be dismembered or broken in two for a golden eagle to carry a piece off – it cannot take a hare, lamb, or anything like that wholesale. The old stories of them carrying babies off are therefore just folktales, probably created in fear of their size.

The golden eagle isn't as vocal as some other birds of prey, but sometimes it emits a high, thin call while flying. Another call it has is *cheek-cheek-cheek.*

Habitat, nesting habits and breeding

The golden eagle can be found living in low densities in the uplands and moorlands of Scotland (the Scottish Islands and the Hebrides) and Northern Ireland; it favours islands and remote mountainous regions, where it can be seen soaring high in the sky. Unsurprisingly, another name it is known by is Mountain Eagle.

It keeps the same extensive home territory year round, and this home range includes up to three nest sites to choose from, as well as several night-time roosts. The golden eagle tends to build its nest (known as an eyrie) on a cliff edge or in a large, tall tree. The nest is a large structure made from branches, twigs and heather, lined with softer materials like grass. The nest is decorated with green foliage, for example sprigs of pine or horse chestnut, which are believed to act as an antibacterial to help minimise germs and pests in the nest.

On clear days in winter and early spring, you can witness displaying golden eagles demonstrating their dramatic sky dance: looping and plunging, over and over. This is done to assert its territory and impress its mate. When the sun shines on a golden eagle as it flies, lighting up its neck feathers, it is easy to see why we call it golden.

Golden eagle in flight. (© paolofusacchia/Adobe Stock)

Golden eagles pair for life and remain monogamous. Generally, it is only if one of the pair dies that a new mate will be accepted.

Eyries can be used year after year, sometimes (but not always) by the same pair. It is added to annually, and therefore can reach a very impressive size. Those found on cliffs can be up to 1.5m across and 2m high, while those in trees can be twice the size. One nest in Scotland, found in 1954, was 4.6m deep after being in use for 45 years.

In March, the female lays two eggs three to four days apart. She incubates these for up to 45 days, starting with the first egg. The chicks then hatch a few days apart from one another. Sadly the youngest golden eagle chick only has a 20% chance of surviving the first few weeks.

The female carries out most of the brooding and feeding duties, while the male provides her and the chicks with food. Then, after two weeks, she will leave the nest to share the hunting duties.

Golden eagle feeding a chick on the nest. (© Tomas Hulik/Adobe Stock)

It is at this time that you are most likely to hear golden eagles: the sound of the high-pitched begging calls of young chicks that can travel over a mile, or adults announcing food deliveries to the nest with a *wonk* or *wip*.

When they are around 65–70 days old, the young golden eagles begin to fledge. However, they only become fully independent when they are around 100 days old. Before this, the adults help them learn to hunt. If you see a juvenile flying with an adult you may be lucky enough to witness this teaching and learning going on: the young one eating what the adult kills (still using its food-begging call of *ttch-yup-yup, tee-yup*) and practising its hunting moves.

Although they are usually driven away from the area by their parents in October, some juveniles stay until November or even December. They won't breed until they are three to four years old.

Unfortunately, 75% of young golden eagles are believed to die before reaching maturity. Those that do survive can expect to live for around 14 years in total. There are always exceptions of course, and the oldest known golden eagle was over 32 years old!

The golden eagle is a UK resident and can be seen year round as it does not migrate (although youngsters may wander).

A golden encounter

Written by Daniel Brooks (aka 'Mullman'), an adventurer and wildlife tour guide from the Isle of Mull.

I have had a wonderful career working in conservation and discovering Scotland's incredible wildlife, but one of the most memorable moments happened back in my twenties.

I was working for the Red Deer Project on the Isle of Rum – one of the small islands on the west coast of Scotland – keeping track of a hind named Germander, who we believed was about to calf. On this particular day I was sitting on a hillside, next to a tent I used to shelter from the worst of the Hebridean weather (and midges!).

I had spent the whole of the previous day tracking her movements, but come nightfall, Germander still hadn't given birth. This morning though, it was clear that

Golden eagle in flight. (© Tony Baggett/Adobe Stock)

THE SECRET LIFE OF BIRDS OF PREY

she had. Watching her through my telescope one mile away on the opposite hillside, I could see that the huge bulge in her tummy was gone. She was grazing alone, not far from the last place I had seen her the night before.

For half an hour she grazed contentedly. Then her mood visibly altered as she started to make her way up the hill. She continued to graze as she went, but she looked nervously around more and more, as she approached the top of the hill.

She was right to be wary. Once she reached the peak of the hill, a golden eagle glided in fast from the right, striking Germander's new-born calf as it stood up to greet her!

Germander ran towards the eagle as it struggled with the calf and struck out with her front legs. The eagle flapped its wings at Germander and the two were locked in a battle for the life or death of the baby deer.

For a while, the eagle managed to hold onto the calf with one talon, despite Germander's efforts. It soon backed off though, and flew away, leaving the calf motionless.

The threat gone, Germander sniffed at her baby a little, then started to graze again. I didn't know if the calf was dead or not, but it didn't look good. It still wasn't moving.

When Germander was about 30m away from the calf's lifeless form, the golden eagle flew back in and landed once more on its prey. This time the golden eagle attempted to fly off with the calf, but before it could take off Germander was back, kicking at it. She was completely on top of the flapping, struggling eagle.

The eagle succeeded in struggling free from under the deer, and flew off again without the calf. Germander once more sniffed at her calf and walked away to graze. She then wandered down into the valley, leaving her dead calf behind. Mother deer do this, even when their calves are alive: they leave them hidden in undergrowth to keep them safe from predators. This time, that tactic had not worked. Had the eagle been waiting for the mother deer to give away the location of her calf? Maybe. Golden eagles are very intelligent birds after all, and use a variety of clever hunting techniques.

Part of my job was to let a calf catcher know the location of sleeping/hiding calves, so that they could catch them with large nets, put coloured collars and ear tags on them, and take blood for DNA testing. So, I talked a catcher into the location of this calf. And as expected, the calf was dead. It had neat little puncture marks through its tiny body – wounds inflicted by the golden eagle's razor sharp, 3in talons, which are the perfect killing tools when grasping prey.

Golden eagles are, in my opinion, the wildest animal in the UK. They wisely do not tolerate the presence of humans, and keep to themselves in the remotest corners of the land. They are magnificent and remain one of my favourite birds.

I knew when it happened that I was witnessing a once-in-a-lifetime experience; and sure enough, three decades on, I haven't seen anything like it since.

Where to see them

Golden eagles live in low densities in the uplands and moorlands of Scotland (the Scottish Islands and the Hebrides). They favour remote mountainous regions, where they can be seen soaring high in the sky or feeding on carrion.

Try RSPB reserves Glenborrodale in Fort William, Corrimony in Inverness and The Oa on the Isle of Islay to get a glimpse. On the Isle of Mull I've seen them flying over Calgary Bay.

Reintroduced golden eagles can be seen in Ireland in places such as County Donegal and Killarney National Park in County Kerry.

Golden eagle with fox prey or carrion. (© giedriius/Adobe Stock)

CHAPTER 12

Osprey

Scientific name	*Pandion haliaetus*
Family	*Pandionidae* (osprey)
UK conservation status	Amber

'I think he'll be to Rome
As is the osprey to the fish, who takes it
By sovereignty of nature'

Coriolanus by William Shakespeare

History and current situation

This large, unmissable bird is renowned for its ability to swoop down from great heights to catch fish with its claws, and therefore considered a great hunter.

Shakespeare uses the osprey as a symbol of power; a power that Coriolanus will embody as he takes over Rome with the same ease as the fisher-king snatches fish from water. Ancient Romans believed that the osprey was able to mesmerise fish, who surrendered to their fate as a result.

Although certain cultures and peoples have revered the osprey for their excellent fishing skills, these skills are the reason why it has been persecuted by humans. The osprey's raiding of stew ponds owned by monarchs, monasteries and others made them very unpopular, and competition for fresh fish meant that it became the victim of shooting, poisoning and trapping.

Because of this, the osprey almost completely disappeared from Britain by the end of the eighteenth century. By the end of the nineteenth century, Scotland was its only haven. Yet, unfortunately the scarcity of the bird at this point only sealed its fate, as it and its eggs became a target for collectors over the succeeding centuries.

Habitat loss, pollution and diminishing food sources are among the other reasons for the osprey's plummeting numbers over the years (as with almost all our native

Osprey flying with fish. (© Ralph Lightman)

birds of prey). The pollution includes deadly toxins within the water and within the fish – human-made chemicals.

Furthermore, the osprey is notoriously faithful to the territory in which it is born. This includes what we think of as unsuitable and inconvenient nesting places, such as at the top of power lines, pylons and derelict houses. This causes additional clashes with humans; the osprey cannot be discouraged from following its genetic instinct.

The osprey isn't a shy bird either; a characteristic that disturbs those who do not understand that there is room in our environment, and the food chain, for us to live amicably alongside each other.

Right on the cusp of the bird's extinction, however, something happened that would ultimately bring about its return to our shores: the early form of what later became the RSPB was created. It initially began as an initiative to stop the killing of birds for their feathers (for fashion), but over the years it developed into the far-reaching bird conservation charity that we know today.

In 1954, the Protection of Birds Act was brought in by the Government, which helped to protect the osprey and its eggs. Then in 1981, the Wildlife and Conservation

Osprey in tree. (© Barry Madden)

Act made it an offence to disturb, take, injure or kill an osprey or its eggs or young, with associated fines and sentences as punishment.

The osprey is still persecuted in parts of the UK, and the bodies of shot ospreys are often found. This is unfortunately the case for many of our birds of prey and, indeed, many animals.

Things are changing though, and have changed a lot. Through good education and conservation, many landowners now tolerate or even celebrate the return of ospreys to their land, as well as all the eco-tourism that comes with that (as with our eagles). One very effective conservation method that has been used to assist the osprey is the provision of artificial nests. This has boosted breeding success and helped ospreys to spread to new areas.

In 1916, the last breeding osprey pair was recorded in the Scottish Highlands – and it was here that they first made their comeback in 1954. During the 1950s, ospreys (of potentially Scandinavian origin) began to recolonise the UK. Fourteen breeding pairs were recorded in Scotland in 1976, increasing to 71 by 1981. In 2001 the UK boasted 158 pairs – still mostly in Scotland (its lochs being the perfect habitat for the bird), but also in England.

The year 2001 welcomed the birth of the first English osprey chick in almost a century and a half, on Rutland Water. This momentous event was the result of the translocation of 64 Scottish ospreys to the reservoir between 1996 and 2001. Since that time, the osprey population at Rutland Water has become well established.

Nests in Northumbria and Cumbria also appeared, and the osprey finally returned to Wales in 2004. Data from 2010 showed 200 pairs breeding in Scotland, and 20 more across the rest of the UK. Right now, there are believed to be around 250–300 breeding pairs in the UK.

Although these very positive steps have improved the osprey's chances, these numbers aren't high enough to take it off the amber list of conservation concern. Larger numbers are needed to really ensure the bird's future, as the genetic diversity of the population at this level might not be resilient enough to prevent it from being completely wiped out by a disease.

Description, characteristics and behaviour

The osprey is a large bird that is dark brown on top and white underneath, with a dark stripe that extends from the eye to the back of the neck. The female is more heavily marked than the male and her breast band is more pronounced. Both have piercing yellow eyes and blue-grey legs. Juveniles have amber eyes and a paler fringe to their brown upperparts.

With a wingspan of 1.5m on average, the osprey is larger than the buzzard, but smaller than our eagles. Its wings are long and narrow, and it holds them in a distinctive, shallow 'M' shape when flying. The female is larger and more sturdily built than the male, weighing up to 2kg – around 14% heavier than the male. They can be up to 60cm in length.

It is the only diurnal (active during the day) bird of prey that feeds exclusively on fish. It is opportunistic and eats a wide variety of fish. Circling and hovering up to 40m above the water, the osprey's hunt begins by spotting a fresh or saltwater fish at or just under the surface. The osprey's pale underside helps to camouflage it against the sky, hiding it from the fish's view.

Osprey fishing. (© Ralph Lightman)

Prey spotted, the osprey folds its wings and drops at high speed into the water. It flings its talons forward, just millimetres from its own head, to grab the fish. Its eyes are protected from the splashing water by a transparent third eyelid. It reaches into the water to a depth of 1m using its long legs, and its scaly feet ensure a good grip. Its reversible outer toe, which can face forwards or backwards, helps it to grapple with the fish. The osprey is the only bird of prey with this toe, as it is an adaptation the bird has developed specifically for this purpose.

It may take several attempts to pull the fish out of the water; the osprey's oily feathers stop it from getting waterlogged. If you see an osprey on the surface of water, with its wings outstretched, you are witnessing it grabbing its meal – which could be a fish more than half its own body weight.

Once a firm grip has been established, the osprey exits the water with a few flaps of its vast wings, holding the fish headfirst (this helps with aerodynamics; see page 150 for a photo), to carry it off to the nest or a perch where the fish will be consumed. Before it lands, however, the bird shakes itself mid-air to rid itself of excess water. The osprey's average hunting success rate is one in four dives.

Adult ospreys do not have any predators in the UK. However, their eggs and young can be taken by owls or other birds of prey, as well as by climbing animals like pine martens and foxes.

When others of its kind are near, the osprey emits a slow, whistling, *kew-kew-kew*. This call can be heard up to half a mile away. The osprey also utters a sharp *chip* when another osprey approaches its nest during the breeding season, or when another is hunting close by. If this warning is not heeded, it chases the intruder away, since it is very territorial.

In the wild an osprey lives for an average of nine years, although it can live into its twenties, with one of the oldest ospreys recorded being 'Lady' of Scotland's Loch of the Lowes, who lived until she was 28.

Habitat, nesting habits and breeding

The osprey's scientific name, *Pandion haliaetus*, means salt, or sea, eagle (not to be confused with the white-tailed eagle, which is also known as the sea eagle!). This refers to the fact that it often lives in coastal habitats, although this is not always the case.

The osprey's life encircles water – whether that's a lake, river or coastal waters. As is clear from the bird's history, Scotland provides the perfect loch-and-low-disturbance environment for the osprey, which tends to nest no further than a few miles from where it sources its food. However, if needed, an osprey will travel a considerable way to hunt at its favourite fishing locations.

The ideal osprey nest is in a tall, flat-topped tree, such as a pine. Providing and protecting nest sites is the main action that conservationists take to help the osprey, since it is effective and easier than providing food (although making sure the loch is clean and healthy is obviously important too). The osprey prefers an unobstructed view, and the best nest site may be used for many decades, growing to an enormous size over time.

Ospreys usually only start to breed successfully from the age of three, despite occasionally making a nest in their first year and laying eggs that do not hatch.

On the whole, ospreys are monogamous, forming a bond for life. They are as equally dedicated to their nest sites, returning to the same place year after year. When challenged, they may even defend it to the death.

In early spring (March/April), the male performs impressive aerial dances, sometimes known as 'fish flights'. This is to mark his territory. Then, when the female returns, it's to secure their bond (or establish a new one). His display consists of dramatic dives of a hundred feet or more and sudden rises, followed by a short hover, repeated. All the while he holds a fish tantalisingly between his talons and call *eeeet-eeeet-eeeet* or *creee* or *creeek-cree*. Alternatively, he may be holding nesting material.

After mating, the female typically lays three or four creamy white eggs with brown blotches, one to two days apart. These are a similar size to hens' eggs. She incubates

Osprey pair calling while in flight. (© Sally Hinton/Adobe Stock)

these for 75% of the time (the male giving her a break the rest of the time), sitting low in the nest. When she is hungry, she calls out to the male with a series of notes, rising in intensity the hungrier she is. The male catches a couple of fish per day to cover his and his mate's needs – when he delivers it, a changeover takes place so that she can take the food to a favoured perch to eat.

The female broods the young once they have hatched (after around 41 days of incubation) and the number of fishing trips the male undertakes is doubled or even tripled. Noisy food begging from the female and the growing chicks is the characteristic sound of summer wherever ospreys live. The male delivers around six fish per day, often caught from various sites, and the female tears off pieces to feed to their young. The male also provides protection from other birds. (It is not unknown for a buzzard to snatch an osprey chick from the nest!)

Osprey chicks grow very fast due to their protein-rich diet, fledging at just seven or eight weeks. For a week after this, they stay close to the nest, practising short flights. After this, they gradually start to fly further afield, exploring and getting to

Osprey on branch with fish. (© Paul/Adobe Stock)

know their home area, and trying out practise dives. They are still dependent on their parents for food, however, and need to put on sufficient weight for their upcoming migration. After they have been flying for several weeks, their mother migrates, while the father stays behind to continue feeding them, until all the juveniles have departed.

Migration

After spending an intense four or five months together during the breeding season, the male and female osprey migrate to places such as West Africa – potentially not seeing each other again until they reunite at their UK nest site for the next round of breeding.

Amazingly, juveniles undertake this journey alone. Fledging at around seven weeks, they embark on their first migration just weeks later, relying solely on an inherited sense of direction and distance. They have to learn to catch fish for themselves on their journey. This unfortunately means that only 20–30% of juvenile ospreys live to the age of two. If they make it to their wintering grounds in Spain, Portugal or West Africa, they tend to stay there for their next spring and summer. They moult their feathers to achieve their adult plumage, and only return to the site of their birth the year after that. Males are particularly site-faithful, and breed within a few kilometres of the place they fledged.

After returning, ospreys fix up their intended nest in preparation for the breeding season. This includes repairing any damage incurred over the winter and scraping out the old lining of the nest cup and relining it with fresh moss and turf, which is kinder to fragile eggs than the material that has been compressed by growing juveniles.

The Manton Bay osprey
Written by Angela Foxwood, a writer from Nottingham.

My passion for the natural world began when, at the age of seven, I found a blackbird's nest in my grandad's garden hedge. Discovering those tiny blue, speckled eggs was, for me, the most wonderful thing on earth.

Over the years I learnt the names of most of the birds I could see. My desire to capture these encounters proved difficult as they usually occurred when I was not carrying my compact camera. As I grew, cameras developed rapidly and became increasingly sophisticated, even being able to make short recordings. With the rise of smartphones and their capabilities, moments like the first ducklings on the canal could be captured forever. However, the most important use of camera technology for me now is the wonderful world of the webcam.

First came the peregrines. Being able to see the fastest creature on the planet so close that every individual feather could be distinguished was something that, as a child, I could never have dreamt of. But the wonders did not stop at admiring their looks; the cameras stayed on them throughout the breeding season: from the first small brown eggs to the first ball of white fluff bobbing out from beneath the peregrine's protective wing. Each year brought mixed fortunes for the falcons; each its own story of happiness, with a few seasons of loss and tragedy.

Later, I was delighted to discover that over in the County of Rutland in 2015, a pair of osprey – an un-ringed female named 'Maya' and a male known by his identifying ring number, 33 – had set up home together on a man-made nest in Manton Bay on Rutland Water. It was the perfect pad for this majestic fish-eating bird of prey, with the expanse of water teeming with all kinds of fish. So began my passion of watching the trials and tribulations of this feathered family in their quest for survival.

Unlike peregrines, ospreys do not overwinter in the UK. Therefore, every year in the spring I tune into the 'live streaming' cameras in eager anticipation of the pair's return from their winter home in Africa, around 7,000 miles away. As soon as I see them, I am overwhelmed with relief that 'my' ospreys have made it back safely. I have come to feel like these birds are part of my family, and the worry when one of the birds is late is tangible, like waiting for my teenage son to return after a night out

Osprey pair meeting at their nest. (© dmsphoto/Adobe Stock)

with friends. Thinking of the many dangers that the birds face flying from Africa to England can be overwhelming.

At the time of writing in 2022, both birds have successfully returned each spring, and within days of their arrival they are bonding once again, long-lost lovers returned from overseas. Sealing that bond tends to happen away from the camera, although occasionally not, causing a slight feeling of invading their 'personal space' while it is still a privilege to witness. The next phase of nail-biting then begins while I wait for the emergence of the first egg, an event that gives me another reason to celebrate.

Over the years, the number of eggs laid has varied, the most having been four. Each egg becomes something so precious that I have found myself heartbroken when disaster strikes. Which it often does. Our unpredictable weather often plays a part in whether eggs and chicks survive, but sometimes there is no apparent reason why eggs fail to be successful. This year, for example, two out of four eggs in the peregrines' nest in Nottingham failed, but I feel happy that two beautiful white chicks are currently thriving.

Back in Manton Bay, when the chicks have hatched, the next phase of worry begins. This is the dangerous phase when all manner of joys and sorrows can occur.

Incubation for the osprey is around five weeks, and generally all chicks hatch within 48 hours. The emergence of stripy brown heads is always a moment of huge happiness for me and the thousands of other webcam viewers. But it always feels as though it's just me and the osprey – my own private viewing.

Once their eggs have hatched, the hard work really begins for Maya and 33. Not only must they keep the little gaping mouths fed, but they must keep their chicks warm and safe. Everything that flies past the nest is a threat and at times I see the anxious parent 'mantling' – expanding their huge wings into a curved position to demonstrate strength – to ward off potential attack.

For the next few weeks, I tune in at varying times of the day to see the goings-on, but this is not without risk. If I happen to see a chick caught in a tangle of twigs, or perhaps appearing to be left out at feeding time, this can disrupt my working day as I fret about how the vulnerable youngster will cope. In reality, the osprey parents are experts at raising their young, and it is very rare for a chick not to get its fill of fish. Indeed, a quick check later in the day usually reveals happy, stuffed babies snoozing in a huddle while Mum or Dad stands guard.

As they grow rapidly, their personalities begin to emerge. There is the boisterous one: usually the firstborn that is always first to the food. And there's the little one: the last born and sometimes cruelly referred to as 'the spare'. Fortunately, during my years of following them, tragedies have only occurred rarely. One year, the adult bird accidently stepped on a newly-hatched chick, which was not strong enough to survive. I cried that night.

Emotions are, some say, only a human thing, and watching the feathered families over the years I have certainly had my fair share, from joy when the fully grown young birds fly off on their adventures, to great sadness when tragedy strikes. But I believe that birds feel something too. That sense of protection that could be called instinct looks very real to me. Feeding, defending and keeping warm involves some kind of feeling in my opinion. And watching the parents looking down at their offspring, I can almost sense pride.

As the babies grow and adult feathers begin to emerge, the chicks turn into what could be described as teenagers. They begin to stretch their wings and seem to marvel at these huge appendages, wondering what they can do. Every day they become stronger and eventually they lift off the nest. I'm sure I saw a look of surprise once when an osprey took its first leap upwards.

The final few days of the chicks being on the nest always brings a sense of sadness as the season draws to its inevitable conclusion. Having survived the traumas of sibling squabbles, fights over food, the teenagers are almost ready to graduate. This time will mean several 'visits' to the nest sites for me to see how many are still there. First, the chicks 'semi-fledge', returning after a few laps of the lake. If I am very lucky, I will catch them taking that first flight, discovering that the world is a much bigger place

Female osprey on nest with two chicks. (© RGL Photography/Adobe Stock)

than the circular platform that has been home for their life so far. Initially, they can be seen on camera, but soon they are out of sight.

It is a privilege, with the help of technology, to witness the stories of these beautiful and fascinating creatures. It has been especially important to me during the last two years, to know that whatever is being thrown at us and whatever challenges we humans face, the natural world faces challenges of its own. We must protect it so that we can continue to witness these miracles of life.

Where to see them

Ospreys return from their wintering grounds to the UK in March/April. They leave again in late August to early October. Chicks tend to hatch in late May and early June, with fledging beginning in early to mid-July.

The best habitats to find them in are estuaries, gravel pits, lochs, lakes and reservoirs. Certain ospreys have learnt to exploit fisheries and fish farms and, because they are not shy birds, they can dive near to boats, allowing for close views.

There are several public viewing sites around the country run by volunteers, as well as specially designed hides for photographers.

As glare on the water or high winds causing ripples make it more challenging for an osprey to see fish in the water, the perfect weather conditions in which to see one hunting is on a still day with some clouds.

Osprey in flight. (© Russell Sherriff)

You will need a good pair of binoculars and, if hoping to get good photographs, a DSLR camera with a 100–400mm lens. From a distance, an osprey can be mistaken for a gull.

Good locations include Rutland Water and Scotland – for example Loch Garten in Inverness-shire and Loch of the Lowes, Perthshire. Osprey-related tourism is said to contribute £2.2million a year to the Scottish economy, and a similar amount in Cumbria. One popular viewing spot in Cumbria is by Bassenthwaite Lake, which is visited by over 80,000 people each year, and Foulshaw Moss. They can also be seen in Kielder Forest in Northumberland (where they returned to breed in 2009) and Poole Harbour and RSPB Arne in Dorset. In Wales, try Cors Dyfi in Powys or Glaslyn in Gwynedd.

While there are currently no breeding ospreys in Ireland, there are hopes that they can one day be reintroduced. Nesting platforms are also being erected in suitable habitat to encourage those passing through the country (on their return to the UK) to consider recolonising their former range.

You can find live streams of osprey nests online, and follow their migratory journey through the magic of satellite tracking.

Useful resources

Websites

www.birdspot.co.uk
https://birdwatchireland.ie/birds
www.bto.org
www.chilternsaonb.org/about-chilterns/red-kites.html
www.discoverwildlife.com
https://hawkandowltrust.org
https://henharrierday.uk
https://raptorpersecutionuk.org
www.roydennis.org
www.rspb.org.uk
www.scottishraptorstudygroup.org
www.wildlifetrusts.org
www.woodlandtrust.org.uk

Books

General
Raptor: A Journey through Birds by James Macdonald Lockhart (4th Estate, 2016)
Restoring the Wild: Sixty Years of Rewilding our Skies, Woods and Waterways by Roy Dennis
    (William Collins, 2021)
RSPB Birds of Britain and Europe by Robert Hume (DK, 2014)

Specific bird species
Urban Peregrines by Ed Drewitt (Pelagic Publishing, 2014)
The Life of Buzzards by Peter Dare (Whittles Publishing Ltd, 2015)
The Red Kite's Year by Ian Carter and Dan Powell (Pelagic Publishing, 2019)
Goshawk Summer: A New Forest Season Unlike Any Other by James Aldred (Elliott &
    Thompson, 2021)

H is for Hawk by Helen Macdonald (Vintage, 2014) – see also the TV programme 'H is for Hawk: A New Chapter' (BBC, 2017)

The Goshawk by T.H. White (Orion Publishing, 2015)

RSPB Spotlight: Ospreys by Tim Mackrill (Bloomsbury Wildlife, 2019)

Lady of the Loch: The Incredible Story of Britain's Oldest Osprey by Helen Armitage (Constable & Robinson Ltd, 2011)

Bird of prey sanctuaries

A short list of UK bird of prey sanctuaries (more can be found online):

Loch Lomond Bird of Prey Centre in Scotland
National Centre for Birds of Prey in Yorkshire
Hawk and Owl Trust in Norfolk
Eagle Heights Wildlife Foundation in Kent
Huxley's Bird of Prey Centre in West Sussex
Hawk Conservancy Trust Bird of Prey Centre in Hampshire
Liberty's Owl, Raptor and Reptile Centre in Hampshire
The British Bird of Prey Centre in Wales

You can also visit Gigrin Farm in Wales (a red kite feeding station): www.gigrin.co.uk

Index